# THE BOOK OF BLACKSMITHING

# The Book of Blacksmithing

Michael Cardiff

Illustrations by Patrick and Michael Cardiff

**PALADIN PRESS • BOULDER, COLORADO**

*The Book of Blacksmithing:*
*Setting Up Shop, Essential Skills, and Easy Projects to Get You Started*
by Michael Cardiff

Copyright © 2011 by Michael H. Cardiff
Illustrations © 2011 by Patrick Cardiff and Michael Cardiff

ISBN 13: 978-1-61004-577-3
Printed in the United States of America

Published by Paladin Press, a division of
Paladin Enterprises, Inc.
Gunbarrel Tech Center
7077 Winchester Circle
Boulder, Colorado 80301 USA, +1.303.443.7250

Direct inquiries and/or orders to the above address.

PALADIN, PALADIN PRESS, and the "horse head" design
are trademarks belonging to Paladin Enterprises and
registered in United States Patent and Trademark Office.

All rights reserved. Except for use in a review, no
portion of this book may be reproduced, stored in or
introduced into a retrieval system, or transmitted in any
form without the express written permission of the publisher.
The scanning, uploading, and distribution of this book by the
Internet or any other means without the permission of the
publisher is illegal and punishable by law. Please respect the
author's rights and do not participate in any form of electronic
piracy of copyrighted material.

Neither the author nor the publisher assumes
any responsibility for the use or misuse of
information contained in this book.

Visit our website at www.paladin-press.com

# Disclaimer

The information in this book is based on the experience, research, and beliefs of the author and cannot be duplicated exactly by readers. The author, publisher, and distributors of this book disclaim any liability from any damage or injury of any type that a reader or user of information contained in this book may incur from the use or misuse of said information. This book is for *academic study only*.

# Dedication

This book is dedicated to my two amazing daughters, who have both helped in their very different ways—Rowan, with encouragement for writing, and Rebecca, whose assistance in photographing a series of blacksmithing techniques proved invaluable.

# Acknowledgments

To acknowledge everyone who helped make this book possible would require a book of its own. Acknowledgements go to my twin brother, Patrick, for his artistic assistance, and his lovely wife, Holly, who made this confusion of words and images a book. Acknowledgments are also due to everyone who has encouraged me to persist, to those who said it wasn't possible, and to those who proved it was. You know who you are!

# Contents

**Chapter 1: Safety** ............................................................................................1
    Safety Equipment ..............................................................1
    Metal Fumes ......................................................................2
    Sulfur Fumes .....................................................................2
    Sparks ................................................................................2
    Fire Scale ...........................................................................3

**Chapter 2: The Blacksmith Shop** ..................................................................5
    Forges ................................................................................6
    Anvils ...............................................................................10
    Anvil Stands ....................................................................13
    Blowers: The Lungs of the Forge ...................................14
    Ventilation and Smoke ...................................................17

**Chapter 3: The Blacksmith's Tools** .............................................................19
    Forge Tools .....................................................................19
    Hammers .........................................................................20
    Hammer-Like Tools .........................................................22
    Tools for Getting a Grip .................................................23
    Punches and Chisels .......................................................25
    Hardy Tools .....................................................................27
    Hold-Downs ....................................................................27
    Punch Plates and Cutting Plates ....................................28
    Bolster Blocks and Monkey Tools ..................................29
    Saws .................................................................................30
    Work Tables ....................................................................31
    Vises .................................................................................32
    Swage Blocks and Cone Mandrels ................................34
    Files ..................................................................................35
    Wire Brushes and Wire Wheels .....................................35
    Drills .................................................................................36

      Grinders and Buffers ................................................... 37
      Torches and Related Tools .......................................... 38
      Quench Tubs ................................................................. 39

**Chapter 4: Materials ............................................................................. 41**
      Buying Tools ................................................................. 41
      Finding Forgeable Stock .............................................. 42
      Scrounging Stock ......................................................... 43

**Chapter 5: Basic Smithing: The Essentials ....................................... 45**
      Selecting Stock ............................................................. 45
      Building and Maintaining a Fire .................................. 46
      Basic Smithing: Getting Started .................................. 48
      Hammer Control .......................................................... 50
      Basic Forging Techniques ........................................... 50
      Heat Treating ................................................................ 59
      Tempering .................................................................... 60
      Annealing ..................................................................... 61
      Twisting Hot Steel ....................................................... 61
      Forge Welding Basics .................................................. 63

**Chapter 6: Troubleshooting: What Went Wrong and How to Fix It ... 67**
      Parallelograms .............................................................. 67
      Getting Burnt ............................................................... 67
      Splitsville ...................................................................... 68
      Cracking Up ................................................................. 68
      Getting Bent ................................................................. 68
      Getting Twisted ........................................................... 68
      Shearly Twisted ........................................................... 68
      Curves Ahead ............................................................... 69
      Hard Work .................................................................... 69
      Long Drawn-Out Affairs .............................................. 69
      Staying Cool ................................................................. 69

**Chapter 7: Projects ............................................................................... 71**
      Punches and Chisels .................................................... 72
      Other Forging Tools .................................................... 78
      More Projects ............................................................... 84

### The Book of Blacksmithing

**List of Figures**

Figure 1. Riveting or farrier's forge ............................6
Figure 2. Railroad forge ........................................7
Figure 3. Railroad forge, exploded view....................7
Figure 4. Fire pot...................................................8
Figure 5. Fire pot, exploded view .............................8
Figure 6. Gas forge.................................................9
Figure 7. Anvil .....................................................10
Figure 8. Jeweler's anvil.......................................10
Figure 9. London-pattern anvil ..............................11
Figure 10. Anvil stands ........................................13
Figure 11. Double-box anvil stand..........................14
Figure 12. Double-box anvil stand, cutaway view ......14
Figure 13. Blacksmith bellows................................15
Figure 14. Hand-crank blower................................16
Figure 15. Hand-crank blower operation .................16
Figure 16. Hand-crank blower anatomy...................16
Figure 17. Squirrel cage blower .............................17
Figure 18. Forge hood made from a water tank.........17
Figure 19. Forge tools ..........................................19
Figure 20. Hammers.............................................20
Figure 21. Cross-peen hammer ..............................21
Figure 22. Using the straight-peen hammer .............21
Figure 23. Using the ball-peen hammer ...................21
Figure 24. Sledgehammer .....................................22
Figure 25. Hammer-like tools ................................22
Figure 26. Vise grips ............................................23
Figure 27. Tongs..................................................24
Figure 28. Blacksmith chisels .................................26
Figure 29. Punches...............................................26
Figure 30. Drifts...................................................27
Figure 31. Hardy tools ..........................................27
Figure 32. Holdfast ..............................................28
Figure 33. Punch plate .........................................28
Figure 34. Cutting plate ........................................28
Figure 35. Cutting plate with hardy attachment .........29
Figure 36. Bolster block........................................29
Figure 37. Monkey tools .......................................29
Figure 38. Nail header..........................................29
Figure 39. Hacksaw..............................................30
Figure 40. Band saw.............................................30
Figure 41. Chop saw ............................................31
Figure 42. Heavy work table ..................................31
Figure 43. Machinist's vise. ...................................32
Figure 44. Leg vise...............................................32
Figure 45. Leg vise, exploded view .........................33

Figure 46. Swage block ............................................. 34
Figure 47. Cone mandrel ......................................... 34
Figure 48. Files ......................................................... 35
Figure 49. Draw filing .............................................. 35
Figure 50. Wire brush .............................................. 36
Figure 51. Wire wheel ............................................. 36
Figure 52. Drill press and drill bits ......................... 37
Figure 53. Bench grinder ........................................ 37
Figure 54. Belt grinder ............................................ 38
Figure 55. Buffer ...................................................... 38
Figure 56. Propane gas regulator ......................... 47
Figure 57. Basic stance working over the anvil ......... 49
Figure 58. Forging an acute point ......................... 51
Figure 59. Drawing stock parallel to the bar ........ 52
Figure 60. Cutting on the hardy chisel ................. 53
Figure 61. Forming a ring bend ............................. 53
Figure 62. Forming an S bend ............................... 54
Figure 63. Forming an eye bend ........................... 54
Figure 64. Forming a scroll .................................... 55
Figure 65. Forming a sharp corner
without upsetting the stock .................................. 56
Figure 66. Forging a penny foot ............................ 57
Figure 67. Splitting hot steel .................................. 58
Figure 68. Splitting hot steel (cont.) ..................... 58
Figure 69. Twists ..................................................... 62
Figure 70. Scarfing .................................................. 64
Figure 71. Fixing parallelograms .......................... 67
Figure 72. Half-round punch ................................. 72
Figure 73. Center punch ........................................ 73
Figure 74. Eye punch .............................................. 74
Figure 75. Slit chisel ................................................ 75
Figure 76. Square taper chisel .............................. 76
Figure 77. Hardy chisel ........................................... 77
Figure 78. Quick tongs, steps 1–2 ........................ 78
Figure 79. Quick tongs, steps 3–6 ........................ 79
Figure 80. Nail heading tool, steps 1–5 ............... 80
Figure 81. Nail heading tool, steps 7–10 ............. 81
Figure 82. Riveting hammer, steps 1–3 ............... 82
Figure 83. Riveting hammer, steps 4–7 ............... 83
Figure 84. Drive-in wall hook ................................. 84
Figure 85. S hook .................................................... 85
Figure 86. Rosehead nail ....................................... 86
Figure 87. Horseshoe paperweight ...................... 87
Figure 88. Heart trivet, steps 1–6 ......................... 88
Figure 89. Heart trivet, steps 7–11 ....................... 89
Figure 90. Heart trivet, steps 12–15 ..................... 90
Figure 91. Single-edge knife .................................. 91

# Warning

The craft of blacksmithing is beset with dangers of many kinds. One is the real and obvious danger of coming into contact with glowing red steel. More subtle but just as serious are the various shop dangers, such as dust from grinding, sulfur fumes from coal, and eye damage from high-intensity light, to name a few. If you choose to engage in the craft of smithing, chances are at some point you will get burned, at the very least.

Protect your eyes! This is a must! A flying chip from a tool can blind you instantly. When you work with any power tool, it is a good idea to wear a face shield. A tiny piece of grit that bounces up under your safety glasses can be excruciating.

If you wear contact lenses, *do not* use an arc welder. The flash from the arc welder is dangerous to unprotected eyes, but even more so if you wear contact lenses, resulting in *permanent* damage to your corneas.

Long-term exposure to dust from grinding can lead to silicosis of the lungs. Keep the shop area clean—the less dust on the floor, the less your lungs will be exposed to.

Never drink alcohol when working. Anything that could impair your judgment will greatly increase the likelihood of injury. Needless to say, a misplaced hammer blow can break bone.

Electrocution: make sure your power equipment is in good repair and properly grounded.

Metal fumes: galvanized steel is coated with zinc, and brass is composed of copper and zinc. When you heat zinc, it gives off zinc oxide fumes. Zinc fumes are well known to foundry men and are hazardous. Steer clear of heating items in the forge that have been zinc plated. If you see clouds of light blue smoke boiling off your steel, chances are good it's galvanized. Steel that is chrome or cadmium plated is also dangerous (especially the latter) and should not be heated in the forge.

If you practice the craft of blacksmithing, you must be aware that in all probability you *will* get hurt. Keep aware of your environment and take every step to maintain the safest shop space you can.

# Preface

I decided to write this book for several reasons. One was the realization that I was finding it difficult to replicate projects I had fabricated years before. I was in effect forgetting the steps in production and having to relearn processes I had earlier applied. And so I began to keep a rough record of my production processes, tools, and stock. I had never been much of a writer, so most of the notes were in the form of rough sketches of the steps I wanted to remember.

Another reason for writing this book was the realization that, while there are many books available today on the craft of blacksmithing, few were available at the time I was learning the craft, and they did not give detailed illustration of the various steps in forming hot steel. What I wanted to create was a series of densely illustrated steps and procedures, with important steps repeated throughout the book.

When I was a kid growing up on the rural Eastern Shore of Maryland, smithing was pretty much dead and gone, with the exception of farriers and a few places that catered to the needs of the local watermen. But this small group was still an industry alive and well at the time, so I was not so bad off as I might have been in a more urban setting. It was at this time that I found myself irresistibly drawn to the craft of blacksmithing.

I cannot, now, tell you what got me started. I had always been a bit of a pyromaniac—blacksmithing, then, was for me a match made in heaven. I suppose I was about 13 years old when I rolled a huge quartz boulder into my mom's backyard. I remember at the time the litany of, "You're going to get a hernia!" (This was a phrase I would hear over and over again during my years as a blacksmith. Now that I am retiring, I suppose it will happen.) With the aid of my mom's vacuum cleaner (the old-fashioned Hoover vacuum that always reminded me of a UFO) set on outflow to blow air into the fire, a wood fire in a small pit dug into the ground, the quartz boulder for my anvil, a claw hammer, and a pair of slip-joint pliers to serve as rudimentary tongs, I heated a piece of broken car spring I had found by the roadside. That day I forged my first knife. It was crude, it was a monstrosity, and it was mine—I had created it!

I proceeded to make myself an insufferable pest to anyone who had the least information on smithing. There were at the time very few books on the subject, and I read all I could find, but a lot of it just didn't make sense to me. As luck would have it, there were blacksmiths working at the local foundry that was right in my neighborhood. Those were great days for me. The owner of the foundry and the men who worked for him were all remarkable people, and I learned a tremendous amount from all of them.

I was again incredibly lucky to have had the privilege of meeting some of the very best blacksmiths on the East Coast in my early twenties. These were people who gave generously of their time to teach and encourage me in the pursuit of my dream. Their generosity taking time out of their busy schedules to teach me is a debt I can never fully repay.

But I can remember, and I can keep their gifts alive for others, perhaps, by teaching in my turn. I find myself slowing down, not quite as eager to load up the anvil and other gear and drive all over the country to demonstrate the art and craft of the blacksmith's trade. It is time to finally commit what I can to print. To keep teaching, if only from the distance of print, is to say thank you to all the great people who have led me here.

# CHAPTER 1

# Safety

Safety is enhanced by awareness and deliberation, practice and good work habits, uncluttered work areas, and safety equipment appropriate to your tools and work environment. However, this isn't basket weaving! You are working with materials that are heavy, sharp, and hot—really hot! Regardless of how safe you try to be, chances are you will get injured. Blacksmithing is like bull riding: sooner or later you're going to get stepped on! Be aware of your surroundings, avoid unnecessary risks, and strive to keep your work area as hazard free as possible.

## SAFETY EQUIPMENT

Safety equipment begins with the blacksmith's apparel. If there is one indispensible safety measure that you must always follow, it is to always wear safety glasses. They are available at many building supply or hardware stores or online. A leather apron, long gloves, heavy leather boots, and natural fiber (not synthetic) clothing are also recommended.

In blacksmithing, a lot of safety considerations come down to trade-offs. It's hot work and you're sweating, yet too many layers of clothing become uncomfortable and restrictive to freedom of motion, and glasses and goggles fog up. Short leather gloves can at times catch and hold a hot spark between the cuff and your hand or wrist.

Thick leather gloves can foster a false sense of safety. Should a glove become wet and you pick up a hot piece, the wet glove suddenly transfers that heat to the hand inside it. Steam is trapped in the glove, and you can't seem to get the glove off quickly enough.

Wearing a full face shield while smithing would certainly protect your face, but it would also become hot and cumbersome, as you are moving a lot when you blacksmith. Full face shields make more sense when working at a stationary job, such as machining or grinding, jobs that throw sparks and grit at your face.

Hardware stores carry a selection of filtration for respirators. Even a cotton cloth over your lower face will help keep you from breathing dust and grit. Once again, there is a trade-off: you may have a top-of-the-line fine particle respirator that you seldom use at all if it becomes too hot and uncomfortable to wear while you are working.

Fire extinguishers are rated for the different types of fires they should be used on (combustibles, liquids, electrical, etc.). Many are rated for two or three classifications of fire. Choose the type appropriate to your work area.

## METAL FUMES

While iron and steel pose no fume hazards to the smith, there are metals that can produce toxic fumes when heated. It might not seem to affect you at first, but be aware that some of these vapors contain elements that accumulate in your system. A few of the most common types you might encounter are these:

- Zinc—This is the material used to galvanize steel pipe and some structural items to protect them from rusting. When galvanized steel is heated in the forge, the zinc burns off, producing a bluish cloud of fumes. As you breathe this, it begins to accumulate in your system. Some smiths are in the habit of burning the zinc off galvanized stock to make use of it for forging. However, I know of at least one smith who subsequently became ill from this practice and later died of complications arising from overexposure.

- Cadmium and chrome—These two metals are used widely in things like eyebolts and many hardware items, but they produce toxic fumes when heated. Once again, I have seen smiths burn off the coating on chromed hardware in order to reforge it. Given the toxicity of these fumes, I suspect this is an inadvisable practice. The same goes for cadmium-plated stock—it's extremely hazardous when heated, and you should avoid using it for forging purposes.

## SULFUR FUMES

The sulfur in coal smoke can irritate your lungs, so it is important to have a forge hood and a smokestack of adequate diameter and with enough draft to draw the smoke out of your work area. Larger stovepipe, 10 to 12 inches in diameter, seems to do this best.

## SPARKS

When you hit hot iron, sparks will fly in every direction, and especially so when you heat steel in the forge to welding temperature. Some of these sparks can travel up to 40 feet. They not only can burn you or cause a fire, but also can pose a hazard to innocent bystanders. They might not be wearing the safety equipment you are and are more likely to be surprised and frightened by a burn you would not even notice.

If you are demonstrating the craft, warn onlookers of the danger. Before getting up to heat, explain the potential distance sparks can reach and urge onlookers, most especially small children, to step back accordingly. This is especially important for the little ones, as they are right at eye level with the anvil and therefore in greater potential danger. It's also a good idea when others are around to announce your intention before you hammer weld. "Sparks!" is the general cry of warning in the shop to alert others who are present.

Remember that on a bright day, sparks can be almost invisible. If you work outside, it is especially important to scout the area you are setting up in before you even light your forge. Remove dry grass to the best of your ability farther than you think the hot sparks might possibly reach. Bright light will also make fire less obvious. You might not notice your clothes have caught a spark until you smell burning, see smoke, or, worse, feel the heat. It's best to immerse the area in water, although you might find yourself slapping out the fire on an ignited sleeve, burning both your hand and the skin even more with the hot material you're trying to put out.

When demonstrating, it is a good idea to rope off the area around the forge to keep people from getting too close. Nonetheless, it is best to avoid the higher temperatures required for welding, especially with onlookers who insist on crowding in for a closer look. Small children can be especially oblivious to the danger. Remember that many in your audience will likely be wearing synthetics rather than the preferred natural materials mentioned in the safety equipment section.

## FIRE SCALE

While sparks account for many of the burns the blacksmith must put up with, there is a rival source for the burns you will receive working hot iron. The oxide that forms on hot steel is referred to as scale. It starts as a thin skin and builds up on the hot steel, becoming quite thick. This oxide flakes off as it is being hammered, leaving an accumulation of flakes on the face and around the base of the anvil. You will want to brush the scale off the anvil face as it accumulates to avoid hammering it back into the hot steel as you work. If you don't, it will leave small irregularities in the surface of your work, giving you a rougher finish.

Scale loses its heat quickly and is for the most part only mildly bothersome. But as these thin flakes are dislodged, they will sometimes, ever so gently, land on your hands and bare forearms, where they will stick tenaciously. There they will fuse to your skin and exhibit the improbable ability to grow hotter the longer they stick and seem almost impossible to brush off.

The thicker scale burns even more deeply and has the added characteristic of being more brittle. This brittleness is especially noticeable as the scale cools, and where it is allowed to remain on the steel, it will pop off as it is hit with the hammer. This can shatter into small particles that can hit you straight in the eye. These particles are usually not very hot, having cooled off, but the tiny pieces, no larger than the period at the end of this line, feel like pieces of road gravel. Safety glasses. Wear them.

Scaling can be reduced by working the steel as soon as it is at a good forging heat. Avoid soaking the steel in your fire longer than you need to, as this can not only become injurious to the metal but also promote more scale formation. A poorly tended fire, where the fuel has been allowed to be exhausted, will form more scale, as there is more unconsumed oxygen in the fire to combine with the hot steel. This is especially true when the bottom layer of coal, nearest to the air blast, has not had fuel added to it. Hitting the hot iron with the wire brush will get rid of a good deal of the scale, as will rapping the hot steel against the edge of the anvil just prior to forging it.

Scale is the likely culprit when you get a burn inside your glove, and it is a good reason to wear leather boots. Low-cut shoes have a habit of catching the hot scale, too. Wearing sandals or, worse, working barefoot will be a brief learning experience for most.

# CHAPTER 2

# The Blacksmith Shop

The shop really is any space where you can conceivably set up a forge, anvil, and table. If it's outside, you need to consider ways to protect your tools from the elements as well as potential larceny. Keep in mind the fire danger from dry grass, leaves, and brush. If in a building, you must bear in mind possible fire hazards to the structure as well as the very important need to ventilate the forge from smoke, especially the thick coal smoke redolent of sulfur fumes as you start your fire. I have seen a smith set up in a tin shed too small to store a bar of steel without cutting it in half. In this small space he had a rivet forge and anvil. He lit, maintained, and worked a soft coal fire in that little building with just the open door for ventilation—he apparently liked the smoke. His was an inadvisable setup, as such smoke cannot be good for your lungs. I suspect that asthma might be the least danger from long-term exposure to such conditions.

I have met numerous smiths over the years who seemed to manage quite well working out of a heavy canvas pavilion tent, but they had to be very cautious, most especially when forge welding, where a shower of sparks could cause an unwelcome fire. Working outside has many additional inherent difficulties, not least of which is the constantly changing ambient light, which can make judging the temperature of hot metal by its color unreliable. The color of hot steel in a shop with controlled light will appear very different than the same piece observed outside in direct noonday sunlight.

Wherever you forge, *always* have some means immediately at hand to douse any uncontrolled fires. At the very least, you will want to keep a 5-gallon bucket filled with water near the forge. You will find it indispensible for cooling tools, controlling stock heat, and quenching work. The fact that it can serve double duty as a safety measure is even more reason to keep this item at hand. A fire extinguisher is another essential investment.

Whether you are set up in a building or on the ground, the following are the basic tools and fixtures to make a reasonable start.

## FORGES

The forges described in this section are the ones most likely to be found in North America, but even within these general types there is great variety. For instance, both three- and four-legged riveting forges were common enough to be offered for sale in farm supply catalogs from the early 20th century. Even the old Sears catalog offered a surprising array of blacksmith tools: forges, anvils, blowers, and so on. There are also forge designs unique to the smiths of Japan, the Maylay Archipelago, Africa, and elsewhere. There are different ways to set up brick or stone forges, some using iron fire pots and bottom-draft tuyeres, some side draft. Some use a tuyere nozzle, which can be a simple clay or iron tube that directs the air blast into the blacksmith fire fuel source from the side.

### Riveting or Farrier's Forge

Aside from the old stone and brick forges, there were more portable types. The riveting forge (fig. 1), also referred to as a farrier's forge, is the lightest of these and most portable. It consists of a shallow, round, cast-iron bowl, looking more or less like a giant cast-iron frying pan without its handle. In the center of this bowl are cutouts to allow air to reach it from the tuyere iron attached below. The tuyere is in turn attached to a small hand-operated centrifugal blower, and the whole assembly is perched on three or four iron legs. If used indoors, a fume hood is attached for ventilation.

### Railroad Forge

Another portable forge—although this is stretching the point, as the whole thing often weighs in excess of 300 pounds—is the railroad forge (figs. 2–3). Again, this is a cast-iron table, but whereas the surface of the riveting forge might measure up to 2 feet across, the railroad forge will be 2 feet by 4 feet or more. This table is bolted to sturdy iron legs, has a square hole cut into it adjacent to the side, and is equipped with a mounting arm for the attachment of a blower. The square hole accommodates a large, heavy fire pot (figs. 4–5) made of cast iron, which absorbs and radiates the forge heat back to the burning coals that it supports. (Important tip: *do not* pour water on a hot cast-iron fire pot; the sudden temperature change could crack it.)

**Figure 1. Riveting or farrier's forge.**

## The Blacksmith Shop

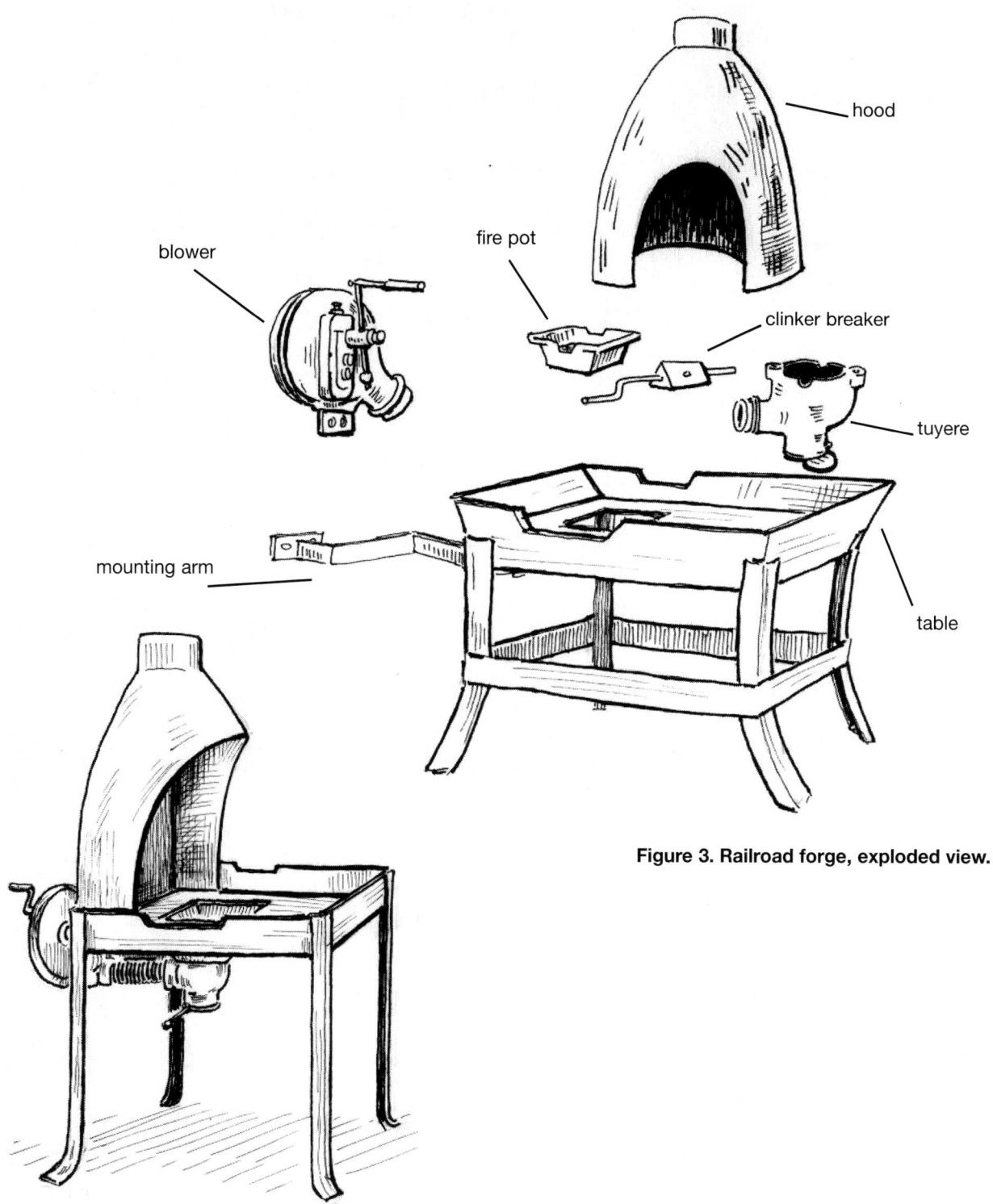

Figure 3. Railroad forge, exploded view.

Figure 2. Railroad forge.

The tuyere iron is attached under the fire pot by two to four bolts. In between the fire pot and tuyere is a long iron rod. Depending on the manufacturer, its passage is accommodated by divots cast in the fire pot, in the joining surfaces of fire pot and tuyere, or in the tuyere alone. This rod is attached to a piece of iron, triangular or T-shaped in cross section, that serves to keep coal from falling out of the bottom of the fire pot, while allowing a generous amount of air to pass through and past it. This is the clinker breaker, and by turning the rod (which is bent to facilitate this action), you rotate the iron block, dislodging clinker and ash from the airway. This allows the clinker and ash to fall from the bottom of the fire pot into the hollow space in the bottom of the tuyere pipe, which has at its bottom a sliding or pivoting door to allow the accumulated debris to be removed.

The tuyere is shaped somewhat like a T-section pipe set on its side. A flexible hose joins the tuyere's side pipe to the blower, which supplies the air blast to the fire pot. When the ash door is closed, the air blows down into the bottom section of pipe, but because it cannot escape easily by this route, it then flows upward through the top pipe of the tuyere. From there it blows past the clinker breaker and into the waiting coal fire above.

### *The Fire*

A blacksmith's forge will accommodate different fuel sources, but a good soft coal called bituminous is favored. There even are names that describe seams of specific coal, coal that has had a history of providing a good fuel source for the blacksmith's fire—clean burning, low in sulfur and ash. Two such names that

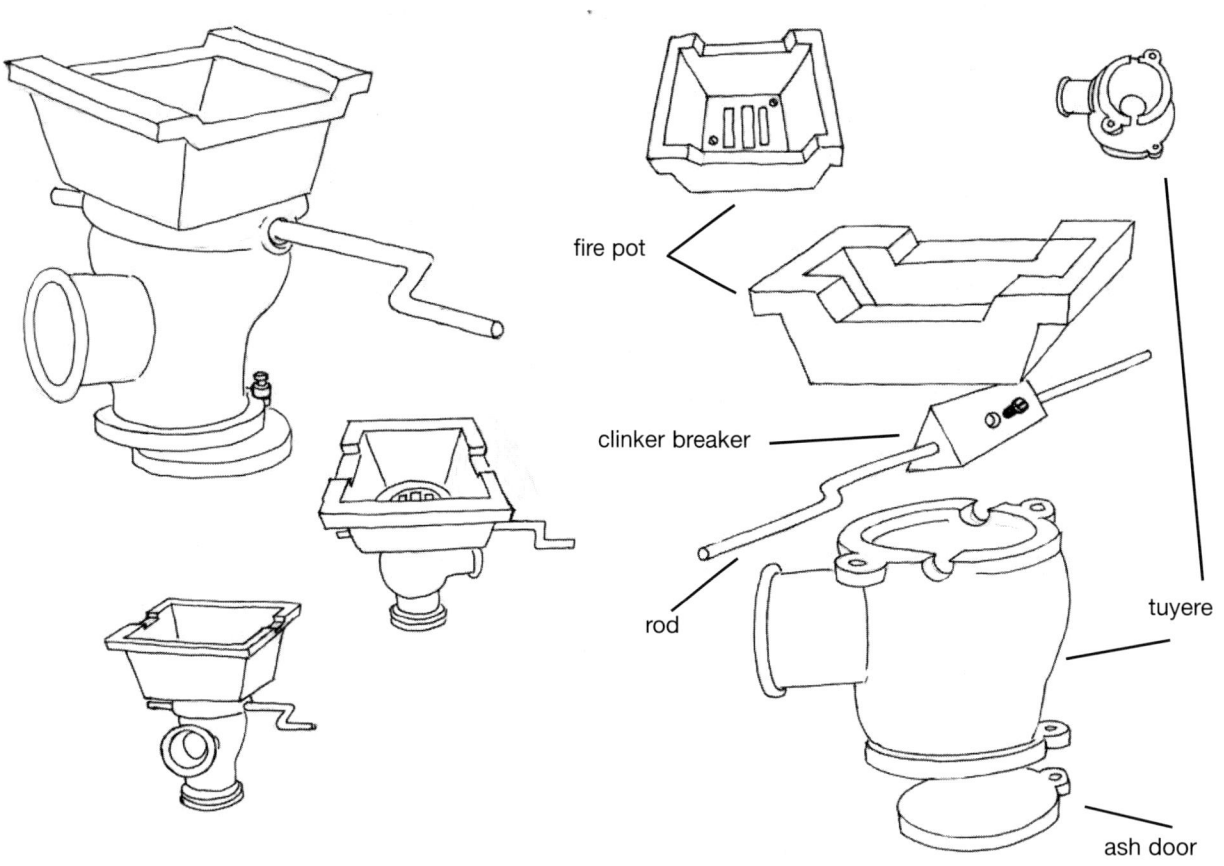

**Figure 4. Fire pot.**

**Figure 5. Fire pot, exploded view.**

## The Blacksmith Shop

come to mind are Pocahontas and Carolina seams.

Coal is graded by size: stoker, nut, and pea all specify the size of the average lump of coal in the pile. Coke (coal that has had the impurities heated out of it in a previous fire) and industrial coke are available in some areas. Hard coal (anthracite), charcoal, and even, in a pinch, hardwood chunks can be used as fuel. I have even heard of macadamia nut shells supplying the fuel for one forge.

The coal forge needs an air blast with sufficient force to quickly take advantage of the heat potential of your fuel. This blast was traditionally supplied by a bellows, which at the turn of the last century was supplanted for the most part by the centrifugal hand-crank blower. These in turn have been replaced by smaller electric squirrel cage blowers. I suspect even an electric (not gas-operated) leaf blower could be successfully adapted as an air source, provided any plastics are shielded from the heat. (More on blowers below.)

With a coal forge, you must clean your fire pot of ash and clinker, retaining all the good coke unburned from any previous fire. When the fire pot is clear and the cleanout at the bottom emptied of debris, you can lay kindling in the bottom of the fire pot and ignite your coal. Dry, finely split kindling will quickly light soft coal with a gently applied blast of air as the fire increases. You can minimize the smoke of lighting up by using small pieces of coke on top of your burning kindling; then add green coal around the perimeter of the fire and let it ignite and begin coking up.

We will discuss coal and building your fire in more detail in chapter 5.

### Gas Forges

Gas forges (fig. 6) are produced and sold commercially, and there are plans available to construct your own. Gas forges, especially those fueled by propane (LP gas), are a godsend for blacksmiths, as good coal is becoming increasingly hard to find.

A gas forge, especially a commercial one, will usually have some provision for self-ignition with a sparking apparatus. Normally there is a regulator knob you can use to vary the forge fire from a gentle heat to a full blaze. The ability to regulate your heat to a specific range can be a great advantage, especially when you are forging several pieces at the same time.

The gas forge, then, has the benefits of being able to come up to forging heat quickly and easily, gives a controlled and consistent heat, uses a fuel source readily available at most hardware stores, and can be shut down with the mere turn of a knob when you are done smithing. But the main advantage of a gas forge is that it produces little or no smoke, which is handy if you don't want to advertise your actions to the world at large through smoke signals and find

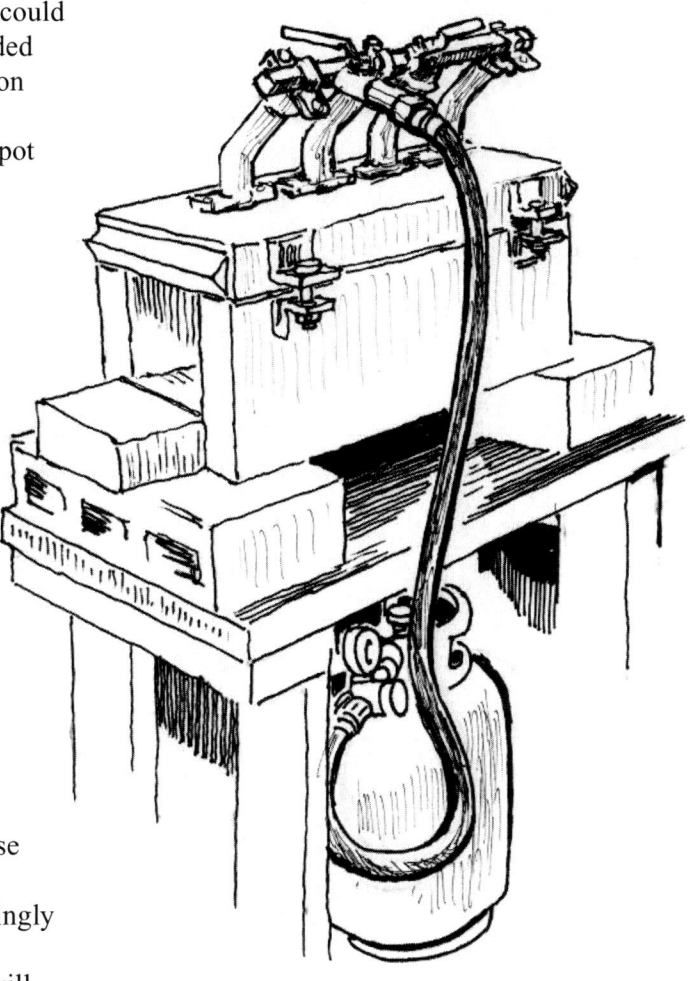

Figure 6. Gas forge.

yourself explaining blacksmithing to your local fire department.

Gas forges have some drawbacks as well. For starters, they are notoriously loud—they have been likened to the sound of a jet taking off. While a gas forge doesn't need a blower or air blast to heat steel for general forging, they often don't quite hit a good welding heat, especially for iron and mild steel. (A blower can be added to remedy this deficiency.) With coal, you are able to exert more immediate control over the fire to produce a reducing or oxidizing atmosphere (discussed more in chapter 5). Plus, there is something intangibly attractive about working out of a coal fire.

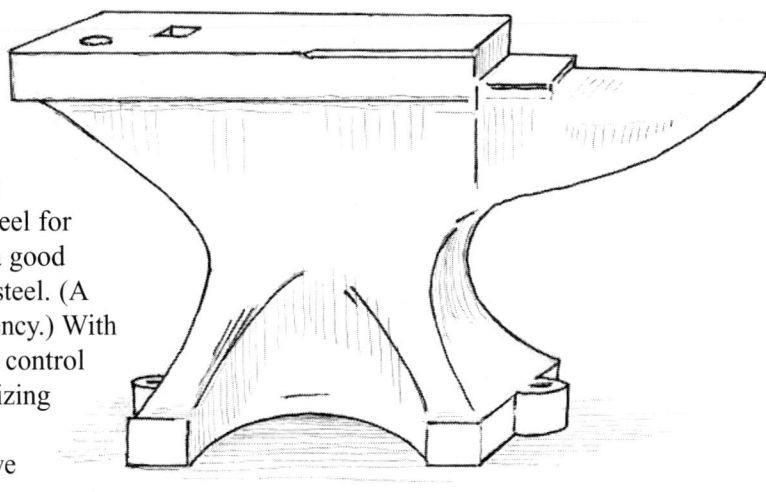

Figure 7. Anvil.

## ANVILS

You have a fire, and that is the heart of the forge. The soul of the forge, besides you, is your next important tool: the anvil. When it comes down to it, the anvil needs to be a large, heavy surface that will resist the heat of hot metal and withstand the force of hammer blows without chipping, cracking, or deforming. This is your platform to shape hot metal on. There were smiths in northern Europe in years past who used large, flat stones as anvils, and there are smiths today who use cut pieces of railroad track to answer the need of an anvil. The best tool to serve your needs, however, is, not surprisingly, an anvil (fig. 7).

There are a number of different patterns of anvils. In the spectrum of sizes, jewelers' anvils represent the smallest, while the largest are armorers' anvils. A jewelers' anvil (fig. 8) can be a simple square or rectangular cube, or it can have one or two horns for shaping small jewelry pieces. The ones I have used have been in the form of a square block of steel with a stout tang at the base. The tang can be mounted in a hardy hole in an anvil, a square steel hole in an iron stand, or a wooden block of sufficient mass to absorb the force of hammer blows on the tool surface and keep it steady.

Armorers' anvils are larger anvils of square design, with a taper to the tail area. They lack a horn but usually have a hardy hole and pritchel hole.

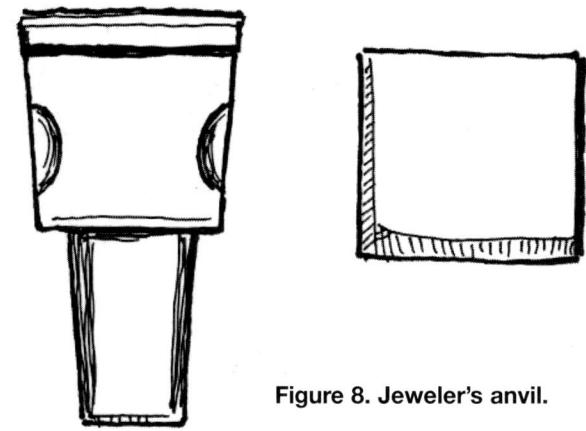

Figure 8. Jeweler's anvil.

Armorers' anvils can still be found and are still in use today, often associated with museum collections or used in the maintenance of artifacts. They are favored by smiths who specialize in the creation of armor reproductions and are purists about using tools appropriate to the time period and geography of the work they research and produce.

There are also double-horn or bick anvils, the so-called German-pattern anvils. These have a round horn on one end and a square taper horn on the other.

Farriers have a number of specialized anvils that are, by and large, variations on the London-pattern anvil (fig. 9). The London pattern seems to be the most common for modern anvils. The pattern features a horn, cutting shelf, face, square tool hole, round punch hole, and tail section. The square hole is known as the hardy hole and is used to secure a variety of hardy tools for use. The most familiar of these is the stocky chisel used to cut hot steel at the anvil. This tool is so associated with the hardy hole that it is simply referred to as the hardy. The round hole is known as the pritchel hole and is used to help bend stock as well as provide a place to punch through hot steel without damage to the punch as it cuts through the steel. The hardy hole serves the same purpose for larger holes that need to be punched.

### Anvil Manufacturers

There are many makes and models of anvils. Some brands I have worked on over the years, and in no particular order, are as follows:

- Haybudden—This is justifiably referred to as the Cadillac of anvils. They are well worth obtaining even at the greater price these anvils usually command. They are very well made, expertly hardened and tempered, and provide an excellent working surface on which to produce forgings.

- Eagle—I have had excellent results with Eagle anvils. They tend to have slightly harder faces and edges than other anvils, and they are prone to develop chipped edges if exposed to too many errant hammer blows. This disadvantage is more than offset, in my opinion, by the fact that the surface of these anvils does

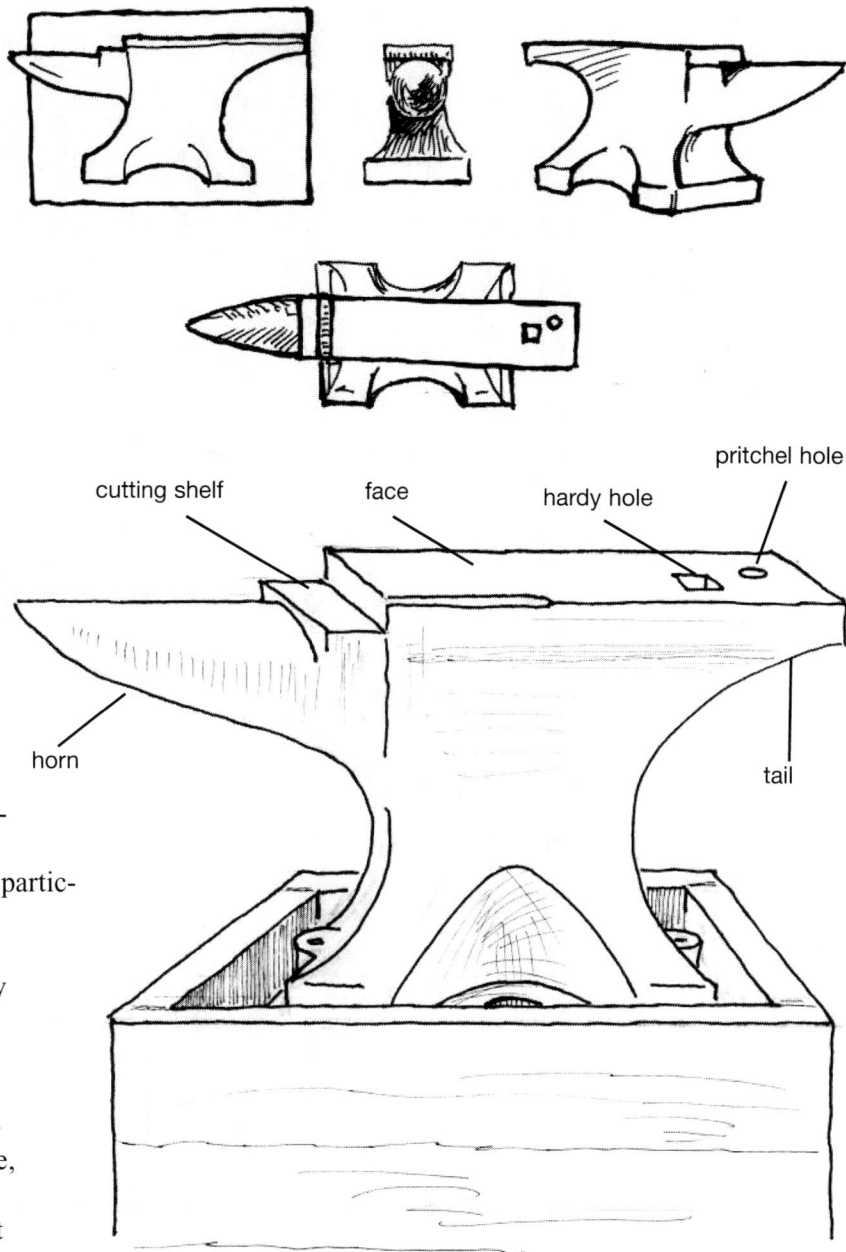

Figure 9. London-pattern anvil.

not become swaybacked with use, nor does it become scarred or indented when cold steel is worked on it.

- Trenton—Trenton produces good anvils, and one I have especially grown to love is a small 80-

pound anvil that is still in very good shape. It has proven to be especially convenient for demonstrations, being comparatively light and portable. Mine is marked ACME in large letters on the side. Maybe it was all those Warner Brothers cartoons I watched, but every time I look at my beautiful little Trenton anvil with the big ACME on its side, I can't help but smile and think of all the times I watched a similar anvil being employed as a potential instrument of destruction in Wile E. Coyote's endless pursuit of his dinner.

This is by no means a full list of anvil brands. Other older models that come to mind include Mousehole, a stocky style of anvil with a short horn and tail section; Peter Wright anvils, more like a Haybudden in general shape; and Vulcan, a stout model with little or no ring (at least the one I worked on didn't). There are many others I am unfamiliar with.

Don't discount antique anvils. The old ones I have worked on were all produced between 100 and 200 years ago—not bad for tools still giving excellent service! These are what I consider the classic anvils, anvils you might find at an antiques dealer or perhaps a farm auction. On rare occasions, even a junk dealer might have one, although likely as not he will be using it. There are plenty of resources for scouting out old anvils. The Internet is a good place to start when searching for these and other smithing tools.

New anvils on the market today range widely in price and quality. Some are prohibitively expensive but of good quality and can be found in farrier supply houses. Inexpensive anvils, ranging about $1 a pound, can be found at tool wholesalers. You must carefully inspect such anvils, as they are often not hardened and would probably require adding a hard surface to give good service. Be sure to inspect the casting for blow holes, which can occur in metal castings. They resemble little air bubbles trapped in the metal. A poorly cast anvil can also be cracked, incomplete, partially hollow, or pitted in the body and face. Casting metal is a craft and science, and the technology is not the same as blacksmithing. For those interested in this subject, there are a number of books dedicated to the foundryman's craft of casting metal.

Anvils are not always a case of you get what you pay for. If you can find an old anvil that's still in good shape, something that has been a working tool these last hundred years, chances are it's a good anvil. If you happen to find such an anvil for a dollar a pound or less, you really should consider procuring it.

### Anvil Ringing and Muting

This is as good a time as any to address the old belief that an anvil's quality can be judged by its ring. It is said that an anvil that doesn't ring will give no satisfaction. I have found that the real measure of an anvil's quality is if it has a good, hard working surface that gives a bounce to the hammer as it hits. I don't know if the ring is a way to test for cracks or hidden imperfections; if so, the Vulcan anvil I worked on, which never rang, also never betrayed any indication of crack or imperfection of casting.

There are occasions where an anvil will ring loudly, so much so that the smith might feel compelled to silence it. One way to do this is to block the pritchel hole with an iron rod. I have on occasion found old anvils where the tool hole had been blocked for so long it had all but fused to the iron rod. Such plugs can either be center punched and drilled clear, or they can be heated with a torch—not so hot as to draw a temper color, but just enough to assist a punch of a smaller diameter than the pritchel hole to clear the plug.

### The Hundredweight

When I first began smithing, I was constantly on the lookout for anvils at farm auctions, junk and antiques stores, and flea markets. Whenever I traveled in rural areas, I always made it a point to stop at such places and see what treasures I might find. When I first started collecting anvils, I noticed an odd thing: an anvil marked on its side 136 seemed heavier than it should be. I later learned that it was! The anvil is marked in hundredweights, and the three numbers stamped on the side don't read in total pounds except the very last number in the series. What you do is multiply the first number by 112 pounds (a "long hundredweight" in the British imperial system); multiply the second number by 28 pounds (a quarter of a hundredweight); and add those two sums to the last

## The Blacksmith Shop

number, which actually is a figure in pounds. So the anvil that I thought should weigh 136 pounds actually weighed 202 pounds! (1 x 112 + 3 x 28 + 6 = 202 lbs.) This would be referred to as a 200-pound anvil.

### ANVIL STANDS

You have your anvil, but you aren't going to just heave it on a table or, worse, leave it on the floor. You need a stand to keep the anvil secure and at the right height for you to work on. The working height of the anvil is, to some extent, a matter of personal taste. A good, generally accepted way to measure the correct height for your anvil is to hang your hammer hand at your side while making a fist; the knuckles should just brush the surface of the anvil.

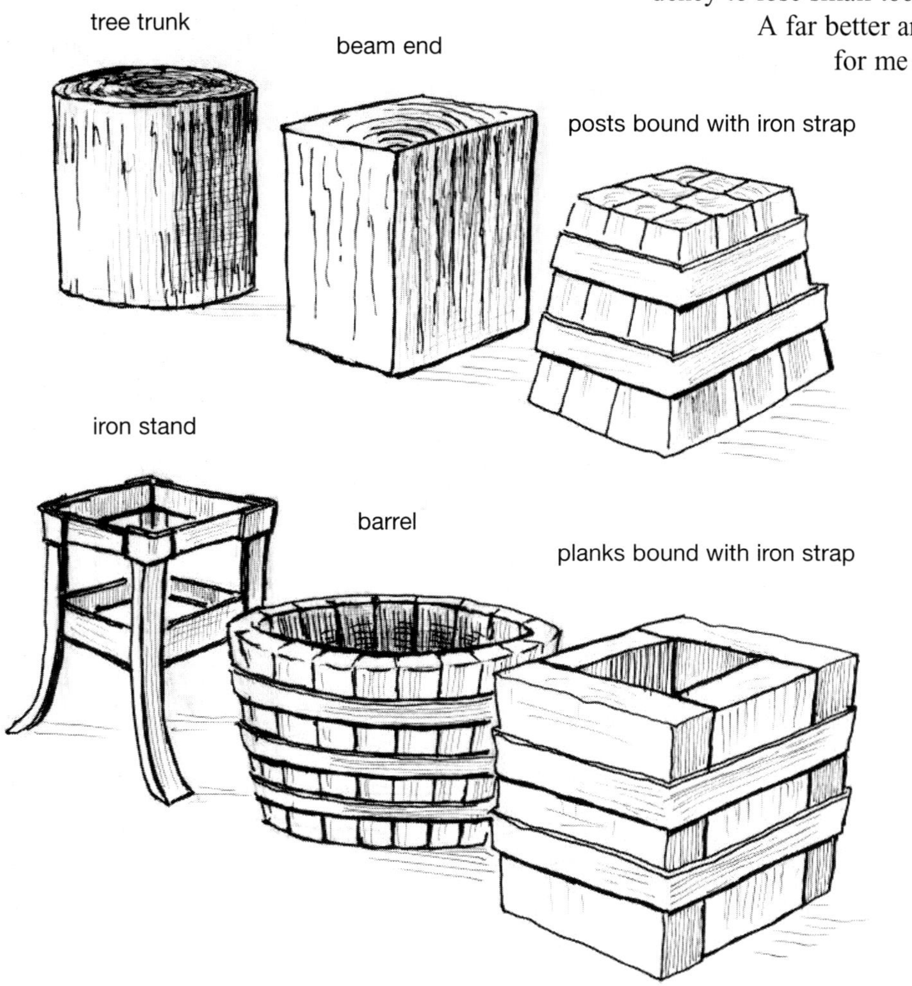

The anvil stand (fig. 10) can be as simple as a cut section of tree trunk or a beam end set into the ground of sufficient diameter to support the anvil base. Sections of log, while easy to obtain, tend to be heavy and cumbersome to move about. Also, if they aren't cut just right, they have a habit of bouncing and moving about. Some people use angle iron welded into a frame as an anvil stand, but I find the arrangement a bit too flimsy. An ingenious idea I have seen used is to take a wooden box or half a whisky barrel and fill it with sand. The anvil rests on the sand and is very stable. Sand is also quite useful for smothering fires, and it's nice to have a quantity of it right at hand in case of emergency. The disadvantage to this system is the dead weight of the sand (making it hard to move the setup), as well as the tendency to lose small tools in the sand.

A far better arrangement that works well for me is the double box stand (figs. 11–12). To make one, nail four 2 x 12s, about 24 inches in length, into an open-ended box. Then measure and cut smaller timbers, a few inches shorter in height, to make a second box that fits inside the first. As each box is open at the top and bottom, cut a piece of 1-inch-thick plywood to fit snugly inside the top of the double box. This is the base the anvil actually rests on. Since the edges form a wall an inch or two around the anvil base, it gives you a place to set punches or hammers close to hand. The interior of the stand is hollow, which not only helps to dissipate the force of hammer blows but also tends to give a positive grip on the workshop floor or the var-

**Figure 10.** Anvil stands.

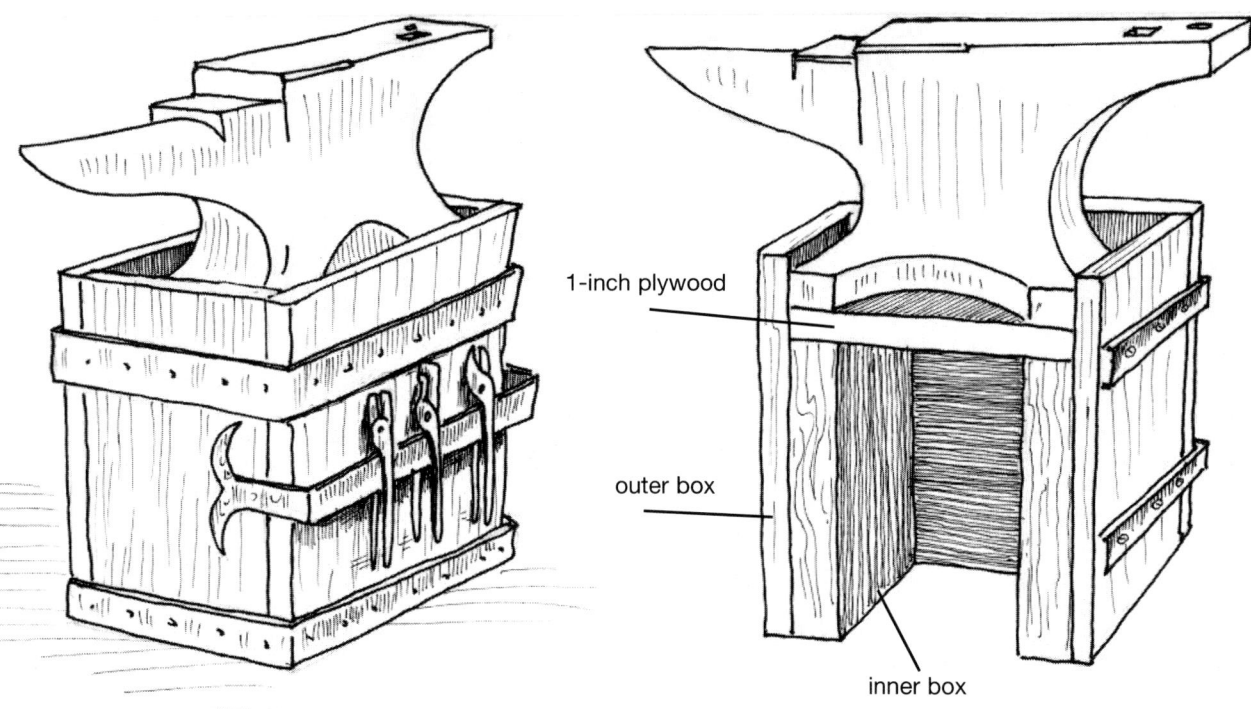

**Figure 11.** Double-box anvil stand.

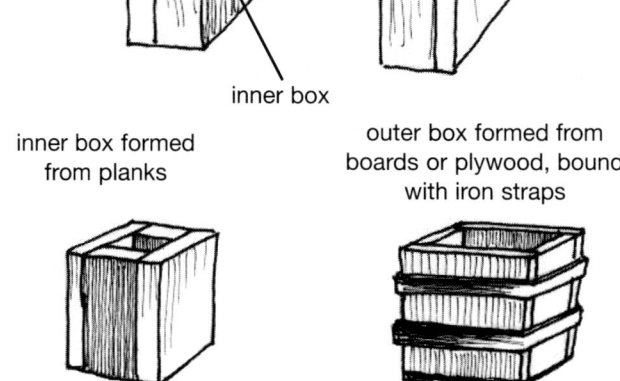

**Figure 12.** Double-box anvil stand, cutaway view.

ious declivities and contours of the ground if you're working outside.

Of all the anvil stands I have used, this is the easiest to move about. The two boxes easily come apart to transport, and they can be reassembled quickly and easily. It is a good idea to secure the wood planks of the outside box with a strap of thin steel banding. You can also use such band stock to make tool racks to hang tongs along the side of the stand.

## BLOWERS: THE LUNGS OF THE FORGE

A basic coal forge consists of a fire pot and an iron table to hold it. To make the coal fire hot enough, air flow is needed. An air blower or bellows is required to generate enough blast to obtain the necessary temperatures in a timely manner to heat the steel you wish to work.

Two companies that produced forges and blowers in the twentieth century were the Buffalo Forge & Blower Company and the Lancaster Forge & Blower Company. Buffalo and Lancaster blowers are basically cast-iron housings with large gears that are turned either by a hand crank, pulleys and belts, or motors. Attached to this housing is a second cast-iron housing, in two pieces, that encloses a fan that is turned by the gearbox. A large hole on one side allows air to enter the blower housing, where it is then directed with great force out of the blower's lower orifice. This is attached by either thin-walled pipe or flexible hose to the tuyere at the bottom of the fire pot and directed to the coal fire above.

Blowers with fans have an adjustment screw that can move the fan blades, but adjusting this screw

## The Blacksmith Shop

too much in either direction can cause the fan to make contact with the iron housing on either side. Make sure the adjustment screw is set correctly. If you try to use the blower with the fan blades hitting the sides of the housing, chances are good you will start to break off the blades. If you hear a clattering noise from your blower, stop cranking and check the blade clearance.

When buying a used or antique blower, check to see if the crank or motor is still working, the housing is in good shape and free of cracks, and the stand or mounting bracket is sturdy. See if all the blades are in good shape. If it turns freely and you feel a strong blast from the end of the blower, it is probably a good bet.

**Blast from the Past: The Blacksmith's Bellows**

I have had the pleasure of working with forges of many different types. My favorite, though, had to be the forge where I first demonstrated blacksmithing at the Carroll County Farm Museum in Maryland. It was a stone forge with a leather bellows (fig. 13) in the blacksmith shop. It was beautiful—the bellows produced a wonderful rhythmic counterpoint while getting the iron up to heat. It was one of the nicest forges I ever worked in.

I set up similar fieldstone forges in a couple of shops afterward and found blacksmith bellows in different antiques shops to install in them. For various forges I put together later, I went with railroad forges with centrifuge blowers. They all gave good service, but they somehow lacked the charm and, I have to say, the serenity of the old-fashioned forge.

The only reason I have abandoned the bellows over time is the cost of building one. This is a labor-intensive undertaking, and once they are built they have to be maintained. The leather has to be kept up, and for some unknown reason mice seem to find them irresistible places to build their nests. It is rather disconcerting to hear a sudden high-pitched *squeak* cut short as you apply a blast of air to the glowing hot forge fire. Nevertheless, if you get a chance to try one, I think you will find it the best of forge setups.

**Hand-Crank Blowers**

The turn of the last century saw the gradual transition from bellows to centrifugal blowers (figs. 14–16). As described above, these are cast-iron housings with a fan powered by turning a crank. The fan speed is enhanced by a couple of large reduction gears in the housing. These are simple, well-constructed machines and, like the bellows, are powered by blacksmith muscle, making them independent of the need for electricity to run them. Aside from the occasional bit of oil to the gear case, they require little maintenance. As a testament to their construction, many of these blowers are still serviceable.

Figure 13. Blacksmith bellows.

## The Book of Blacksmithing

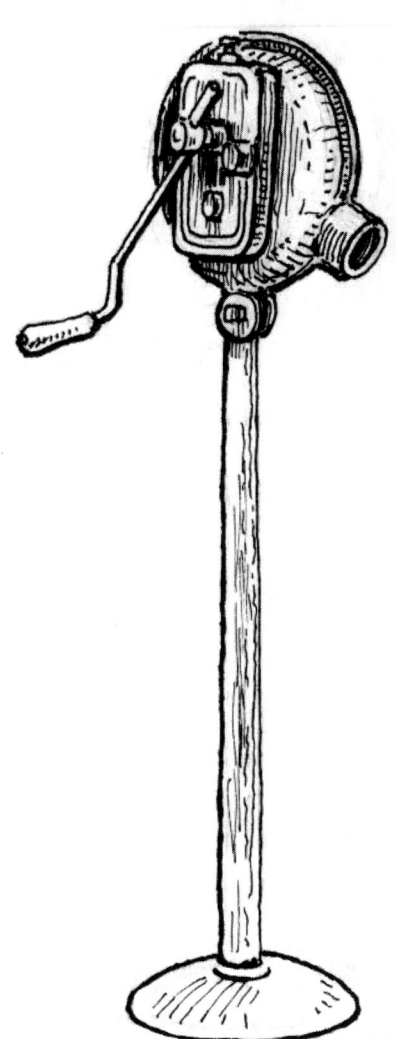

Figure 14. Hand-crank blower.

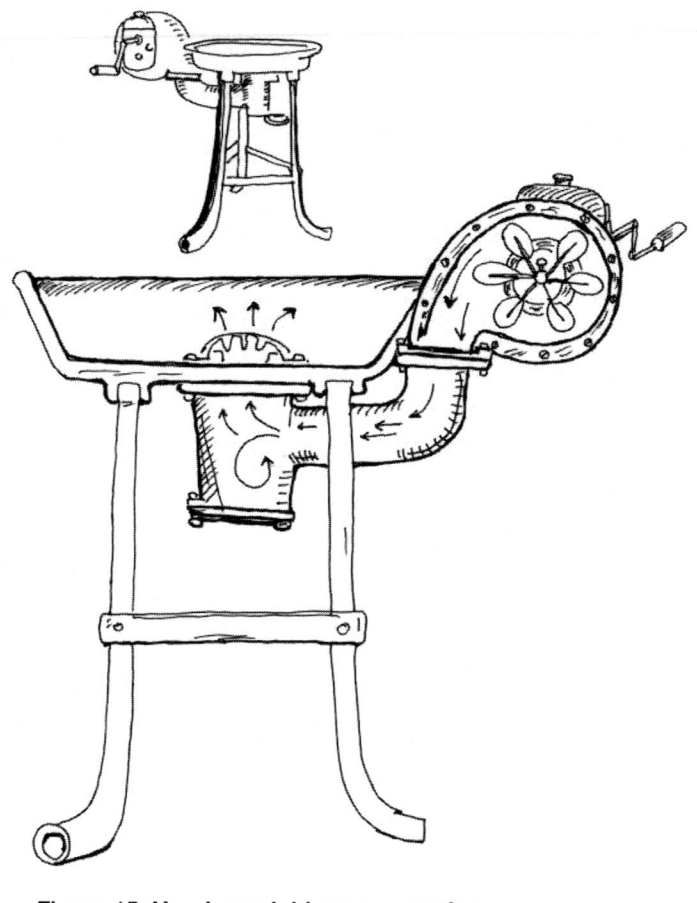

Figure 15. Hand-crank blower operation.

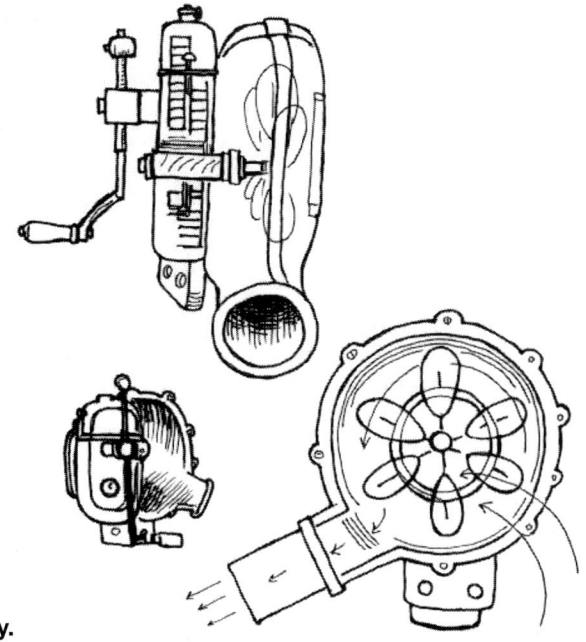

Figure 16. Hand-crank blower anatomy.

## The Blacksmith Shop

**Squirrel Cage Blowers**

Many new blowers are of the squirrel cage type (fig. 17), with the fan blades set in a cage rather reminiscent of a hamster exercise wheel. They are run off electricity and need either a rheostat or sliding door arrangement to limit and control the blast of air supplied to the fire, thus making the heat of the fire manageable. Any sufficient source of forced air will do the job. Metal flex hoses used for clothes dryers are an excellent means of getting your air safely to your fire while keeping you and your blower a reasonable distance from the heat.

### VENTILATION AND SMOKE

Some farrier supply companies, such as Centaur Forge, sell forge hoods. Stainless steel hoods are more expensive but last considerably longer. You can also make your own from 10- to 12-gauge steel sheet.

I made my forge hood out of a water pressure reservoir tank I found in a salvage yard (fig. 18). I used a Sawzall tool to cut a 10-inch hole in its hemispherical top to accommodate my smokestack. I then cut the bottom off the tank, leaving me with a metal shell of 10-gauge steel measuring 7 feet around and about 3 feet tall. Finally, I cut a 14- x 18-inch door with a rounded top into the front.

This forge hood produces a swirling smoke that spirals up into the smokestack and has proved to be the best smoke-venting hood I have ever used. I kept the steel from the door cutout, and I use it when first starting the fire on those days when the prevailing winds backdraft the smoke. Once the fire is hot, though, this hood and stack combination works marvelously.

Iron stovepipe can be found in hardware stores and places that deal in woodstoves. The black iron stovepipe is least expensive but requires regular replacement, as the forge smoke corrodes it. It eventually rusts out and allows smoke to leak into the shop. Stainless steel stovepipe is more expensive but lasts much longer, offsetting its greater expense with longer intervals between replacements.

Stovepipe can be single or double wall, depending on the shop you're working in. Double wall, while more expensive, is safer. Should the pipe overheat, it is less of a fire hazard to your building.

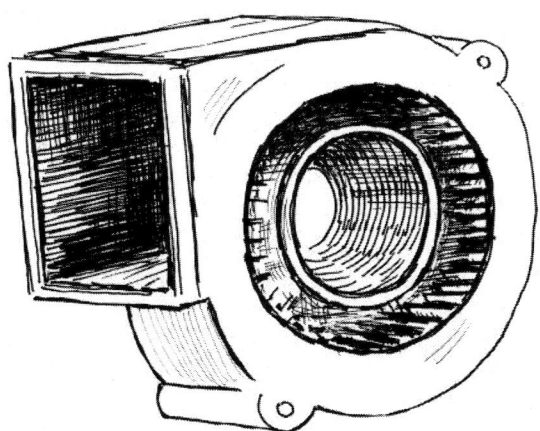

Figure 17. Squirrel cage blower.

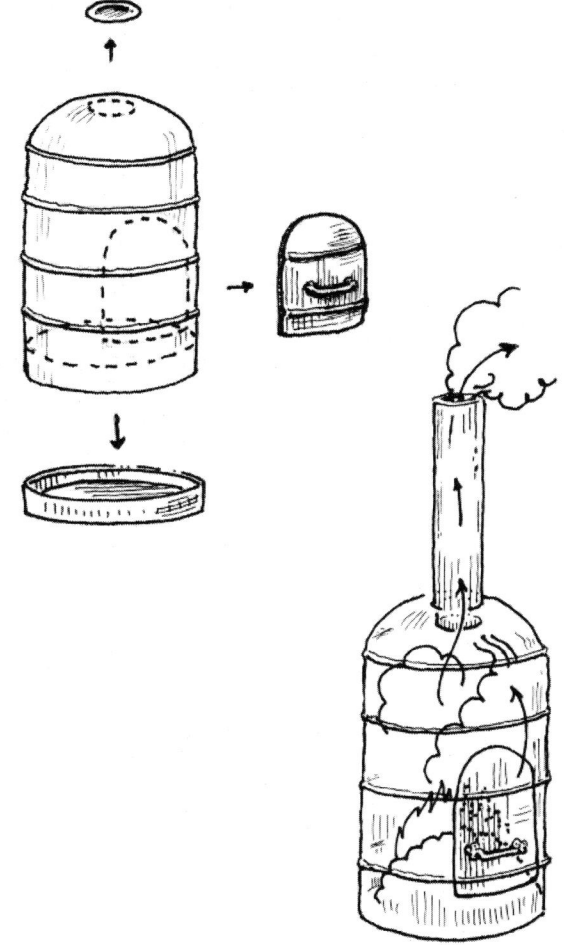

Figure 18. Forge hood made from a water tank.

# CHAPTER 3

# The Blacksmith's Tools

You have a forge, a blower, and an anvil. Now you need something to hit with, hold with, cut with, shape with, grind with—all the myriad processes involved in manipulating hot iron—and for this you will need tools! Hammers are used for moving, bending, and shaping metal. Vises and tongs give leverage and hold hot metal. Punches, chisels, and swages cut and shape the work further, and grinders and files allow fine shaping and finishing.

There is a seemingly endless variety of tools used in smithing. Many are very specialized in their function and use. While it may be tempting to acquire all the different types available, it's probably better to start with the basic tools and add to these as need and opportunity allow.

## FORGE TOOLS

You should have a few tools near the forge to help you manipulate and control your fire (fig. 19).

A poker can be as simple as a piece of 5/16- or 3/8-inch round stock with a loop or hook at the end of the handle to hang it from and a tapered point to perform such routine tasks as clearing airways, breaking up clinkers, and creating spy holes in the hot coals to look at the progress of iron that you're heating.

The rake is a little bit larger stock, as it is used to pull coal into the fire from the sides as it cokes up. It can also be used to scoop out clinker and ash from the bottom of the fire pot while working. Its working end is a flattened hook with a shallow bend to help sweep your fuel to where you want to move it.

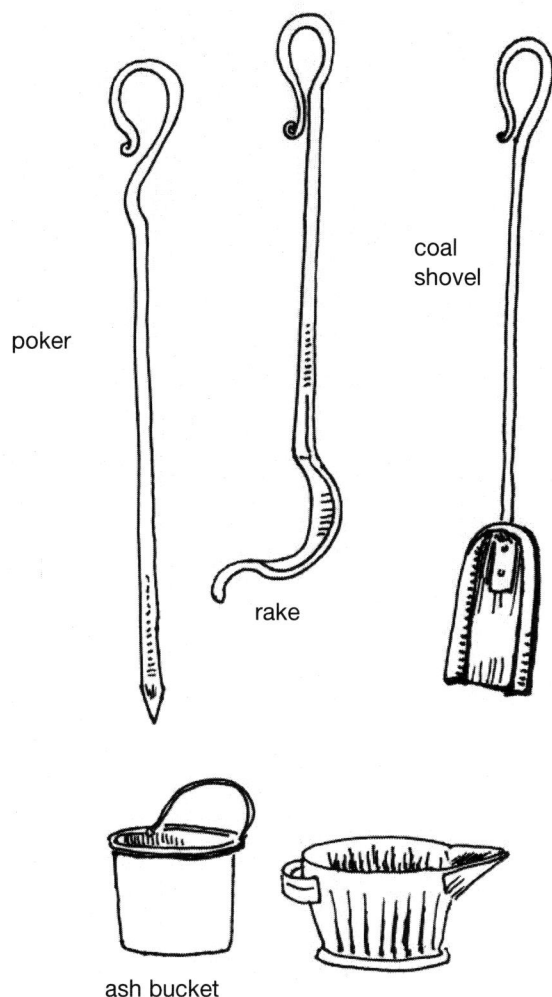

Figure 19. Forge tools.

A small shovel is used to scoop coal into the fire and is useful at the end of the day when you clean out coke, ash, and clinker from the fire pot.

A metal bucket placed under the ash cleanout at the bottom of the fire pot allows you to dump the hot ash and clinkers from the bottom of the tuyere as you're working and keeps the shop clear of the refuse.

A coal scuttle is a metal bucket with a projecting lip that allows you to keep coal stored near the fire as you work.

## HAMMERS

Hammers (fig. 20) are as basic to smithing as fire, anvil, and tongs. Your hammer weight should be whatever weight is most comfortable for you to wield and still adequately move the size stock you wish to forge. Thus lighter hammers are best employed for small stock, whereas heavier hammers are needed to move larger stock. Hammers for smithing generally range from 1 to 5 pounds. As you smith, you will probably come to prefer heavier hammers as you build strength and endurance to move metal more quickly and efficiently. Length of handle seems a personal preference, but you want enough length to generate a certain spring to the hammer blow to transfer the potential energy of the blow more efficiently to the hot iron.

The face of your hammer is used to shape and flatten steel. The force of the blow disperses in multiple directions, moving the steel both lengthwise and widthwise as it is reduced in cross section when hit by the hammer face.

The peen, the end opposite to the

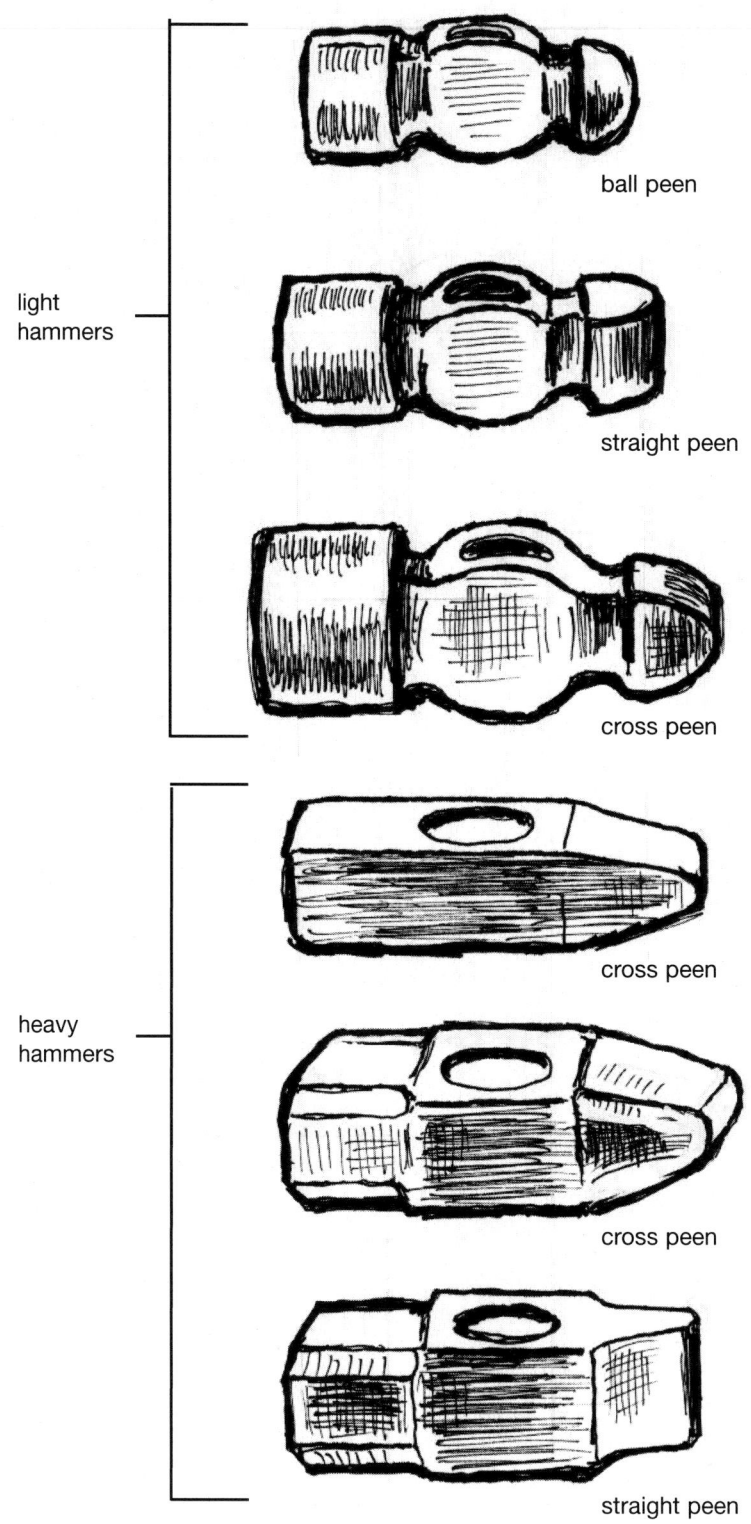

Figure 20. Hammers.

## The Blacksmith's Tools

hammer face, is a tapered wedge that allows the smith to move stock in a specific direction. It is, in effect, a hand-operated fuller. (More on fullers below.)

Your hammer face leaves its mark on the metal, and imperfections like dents, chips, and sharp edges will mar the surface of the iron you are working on. Here the jewelers are on to something. Jewelers take great pains to keep their hammer faces polished so as to leave the surface of their work clean of imperfections. Therefore, it is worth your while to keep your hammer face in good repair to save yourself needless finishing work, cleaning a surface later with files that you might have otherwise hammered smooth. Polish at least one or two of your hammer faces and leave these aside for your finishing work. Use another hammer for striking other tools like punches and chisels.

Hammer handles are best made from hard, tough, springy wood like ash, hickory, white oak, or Osage, to name a few. Be sure to keep your hammer handles in good repair, and replace any that have developed cracks or splits. Keep your hammer heads tightly wedged to the handle with wooden or metal wedges. I have had good results with a section of 5/16-inch iron pipe as a wedge. Cut a short section with one end at a 45-degree taper. Once hammered into the handle, it swells the wood around the top of the tool, creating a positive attachment of head to handle.

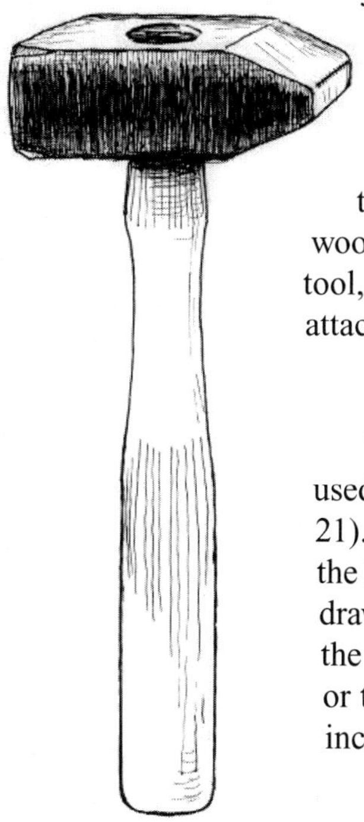

### Cross Peen

This is the hammer most used by the blacksmith (fig. 21). The peen is transverse to the handle and is used to draw the steel crosswise to the stock—that is, to widen or taper the stock without increasing it in length.

Figure 21. Cross-peen hammer.

### Straight Peen

This hammer is used like the cross peen except that the peen is in line with the hammer handle. It is used to draw stock lengthwise without appreciably widening it at the same time (fig. 22).

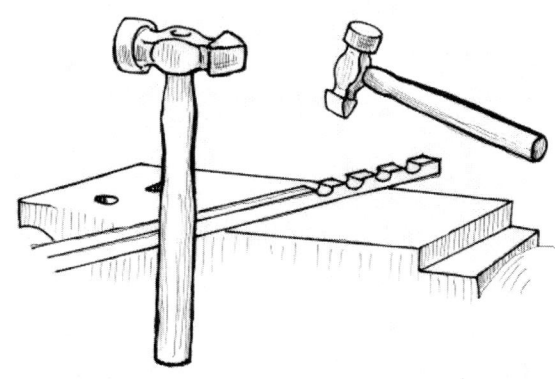

Figure 22. Using the straight-peen hammer.

### Ball Peen

The ball peen is more a machinist's than a blacksmith's hammer, but it is used to form hollows and rivet heads (fig. 23).

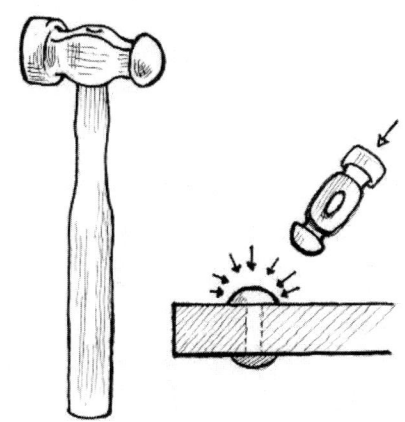

Figure 23. Using the ball-peen hammer.

21

## The Book of Blacksmithing

### Sledge

The sledgehammer (fig. 24) is the heavy hitter of blacksmith hammers and can be anywhere from 5 to more than 20 pounds in weight. Its defining characteristic is its handle, which is much longer than a normal smith hammer handle, allowing the striker to use both hands to wield and control it.

### HAMMER-LIKE TOOLS

Hammer-like tools (fig. 25) are easily mistaken for hammers. They are set at the end of a handle that allows them to be held and in some cases swung in a hammer-like manner. However, many of these tools are actually designed to be laid on the work and struck by a hammer. The handle is not designed to be swung but to serve as a means to hold the tool in place. As a group they are known as top tools, whereas bottom tools are stationary, usually secured to the anvil by a square shank set into the hardy hole. The stock is then shaped between the top tool and the bottom tool.

### Set Hammers

This tool looks like a small, square hammer with

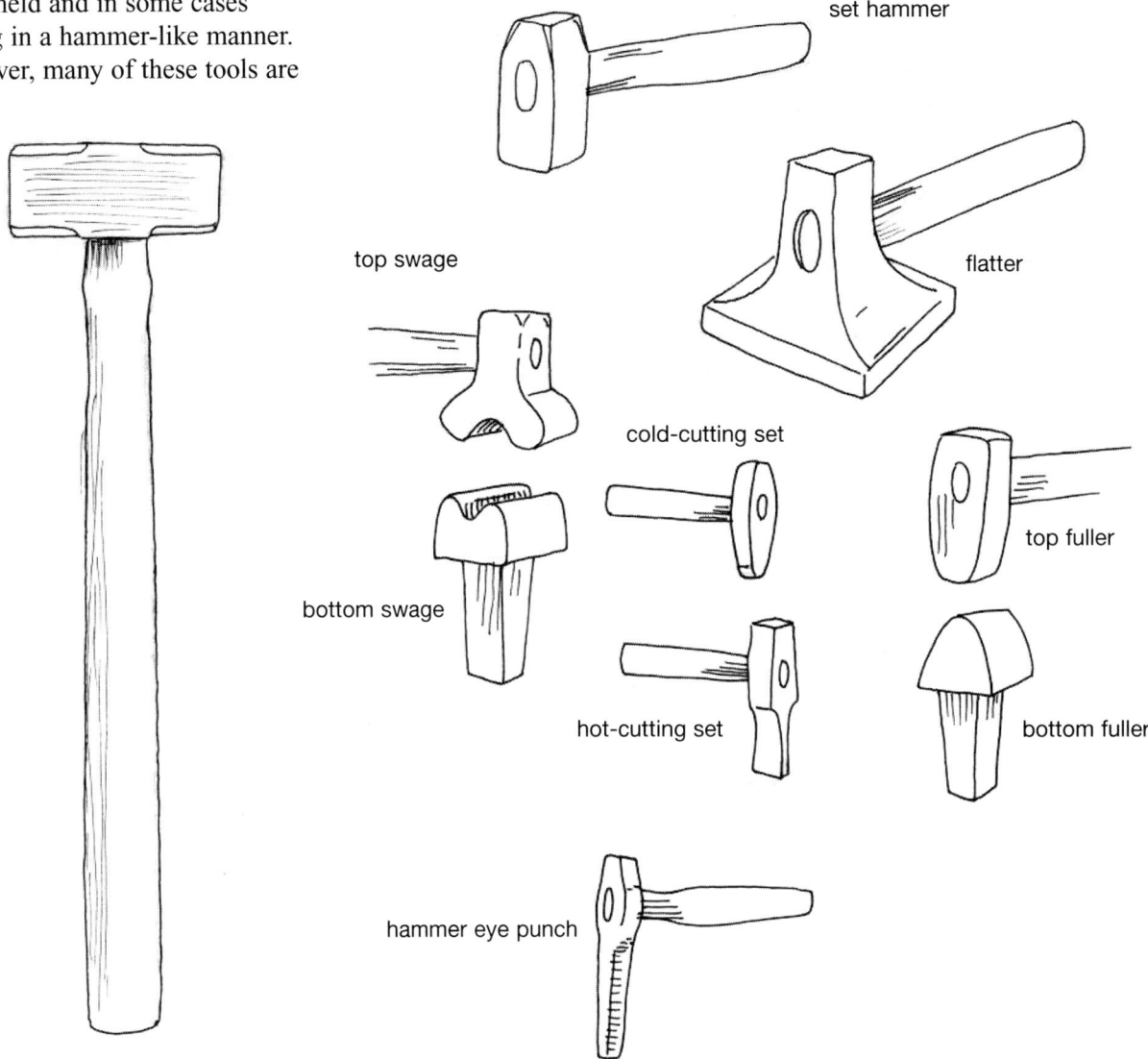

Figure 24. Sledgehammer.

Figure 25. Hammer-like tools.

slightly rounded edges. It is used with the aid of a striker (i.e., assistant, often an apprentice) or, lacking that, a hold-down to keep your stock steady as you work it. It is used to forge in tight areas and to develop sharp shoulders in forged work.

### Flatters

These are shaped like set hammers but with a face that is much wider, flared out from ½ to 1 inch broader than the face of the set hammer. About ½ inch in thickness, its function is to disperse the force of the hammer blows and give a smooth, even surface to iron work. Like all these handled tools, it requires a third hand—either a striker to assist the blacksmith or, once again, some system of holding the stock you are working on.

### Fullers

These are similar to straight-peen hammers in that their working edge is in line with the handle. They can be narrow to very broad, with their working edge half round, like a blunt chisel edge. They are used to fuller stock (i.e., to draw stock in a specific direction) or to divot the stock.

### Top Sets

Basically like the set hammer in shape, top sets come in a nearly infinite number of forms to shape iron in cross section. They can be used in conjunction with bottom tools or a swage block to form round stock, angles, finials, etc.

### Cold-Cutting Set

This tool performs a similar function as the cold-cutting hardy chisel, being a handled chisel with an acute edge to allow for the rigors of cutting cold steel, similar in shape to the fuller but with a sharp edge. It can be used in conjunction with a bottom hardy tool or with a cutting plate beneath it. Cutting steel with this chisel on the anvil face is inadvisable, as the hardened cutting edge might mar the anvil or damage the chisel's edge if it were to cut all the way through the stock. Usually, nicking the stock deeply on all sides will allow you to break it off over the edge of the anvil.

### Hot-Cutting Set

Like the cold chisel but less robust, it has a thinner blade with a sharp edge and cuts through hot steel quickly and much more easily than a cold set can. It should be used to cut hot steel only, as its temper will be drawn from contact with the hot steel, making it unsuitable for cutting cold stock. As with the cold cutter, it is best to work over an iron plate if you are intending to cut all the way through the steel to avoid damage to the anvil and the hot set edge.

### Hammer Eye Punch

This is a robust punch, usually round in cross section, with a slight taper and flat end. It is used to punch through large stock when forming the eye for the handle of things like hammers and hammer tools.

## TOOLS FOR GETTING A GRIP

When hitting things, you generally want them to hold still. When holding hot things, you don't want to drop them. When you do these things together, it's vital that you have a secure grip on your work, and this is where vise grips, crescent wrenches, and tongs come in. Different shaped stock and different jobs will call for different tools, so choose accordingly. If the tool doesn't offer a secure hold, you may endanger your work and yourself.

### Vise Grips

Vise grips (fig. 26) are handy tools to have in the shop. They come in numerous sizes, and it is good to keep a selection so you can firmly grip smaller items that need to be worked on power tools.

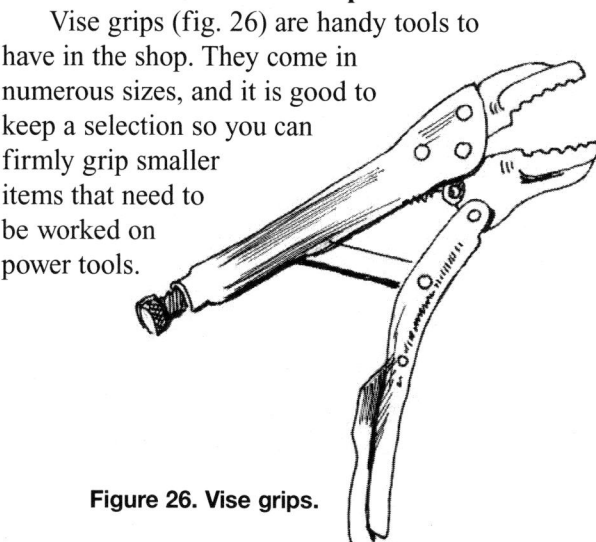

Figure 26. Vise grips.

## Crescent Wrenches

Crescent wrenches have adjustable jaws and come in handy for gripping stock for twisting. The stock is held securely in a vise and the jaws adjusted to slide onto and off the work as it is being twisted. When twisting hot steel, avoid rotating so far that your hand is under the hot work being twisted, as scale will be dislodged and will land on your hand and wrist.

## Tongs

Tongs are the pliers-like tool with which the blacksmith grips hot iron (fig. 27). Tongs come in a nearly infinite range of sizes, shapes, rein length, and jaw shape. Using the right pair for the work to be held is vital to the safety of the smith (and any bystanders). There are few things more disconcerting

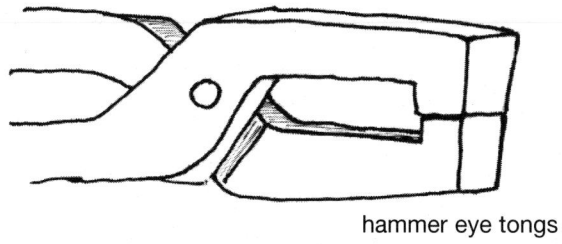
hammer eye tongs

pick-up tongs

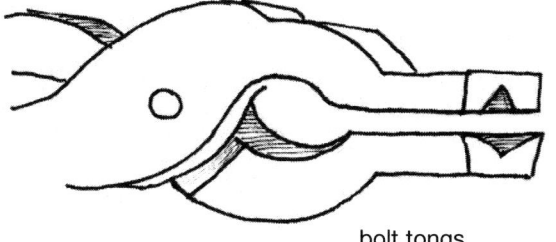
bolt tongs

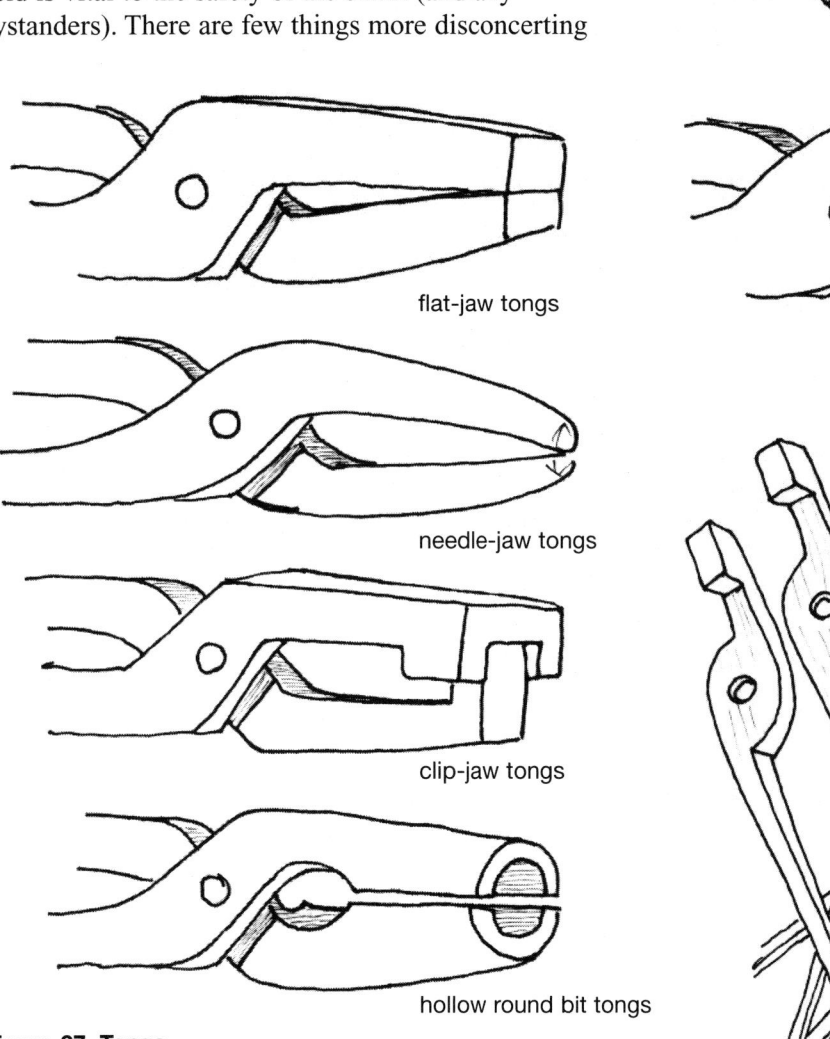

flat-jaw tongs

needle-jaw tongs

clip-jaw tongs

hollow round bit tongs

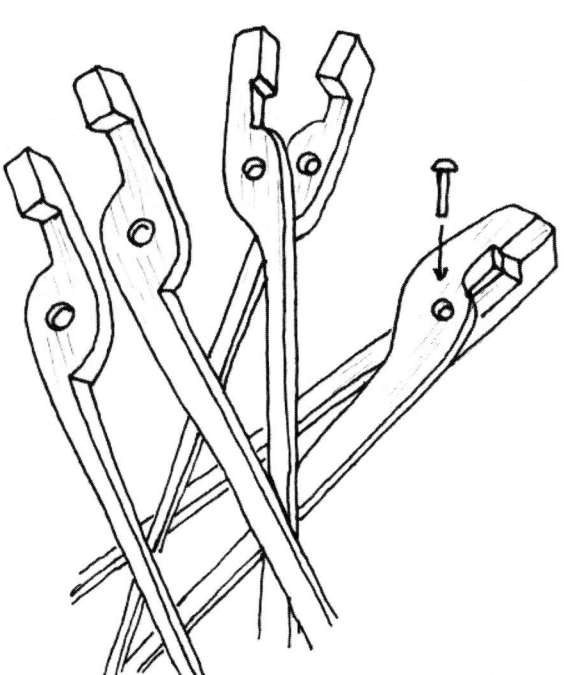

**Figure 27. Tongs.**

than seeing a red-hot piece of steel spinning before your eyes, yet this is exactly what can happen if you hit a piece of work held by the insecure grip supplied by the wrong tongs for the job.

Lighter tongs give a good grip on small stock and are less fatiguing to hold, but larger stock is better held by tongs with more mass. Long handles (reins) keep you out of the fire, but the length of the tongs really is a matter of personal preference. Unless I am working a very hot fire for welding or working with very large sections of stock, I mostly use tongs with comparatively short handles. Use what suits you best. One of the nicest things about being a blacksmith is being able to make your own to tools to fit your specific needs.

Tongs are necessary to hold short sections of hot steel securely for hammering and shaping, but when working with longer stock, they might not be necessary. Bars of steel from 2 to 3 feet don't heat up toward the end you're holding, at least not very quickly, and holding the bar in your hand does afford an unequaled grip. When making small items like nails, for instance, it is customary to work directly off the longer bar, forging the nail as close to finished as possible before nicking the stock and securing it in a nail-heading tool to finish the nail head, thus relieving the smith of attempting to manipulate a small piece of iron with tongs. Small pieces are easily lost in the bottom of the fire and burned.

The tongs that see the most use in my shop are the following:

- Flat-jaw tongs—The most common tong jaws are flat jaws. They are easily reheated to conform to the shape of stock you want to form. Flat-jaw tongs are often the primary shape that other tongs are derived from. They will adequately hold flat stock but are less secure on stock that does not have flat surfaces.

- Needle-jaw tongs—Also called scrolling tongs, these tongs look a bit like large needle-nose pliers. The bits have round cross sections, tapering to a point, and are useful for bending stock and forming scrolls.

- Clip-jaw tongs—These tongs are shaped like flat-jaw tongs, with one of the jaws having a slightly wider jaw with protrusions that help to secure flat stock and resist lateral movement. These tongs afford a very secure grip when they are of a size to match the flat stock they are intended to hold.

- Hollow round bit tongs—Like clip tongs, these afford an excellent grip on stock, having a hollow cavity that helps prevent lateral motion. They are especially suited to holding stock of round or square cross section.

- Hammer eye tongs—Hammer eye tongs have jaws whose ends are bent at an angle toward one another. This shape allows you to hold pierced stock firmly. These tongs are ideally suited to gripping hammerheads and similar work after the eye has been forged into them. The bent ends of the jaws fit from above and below into the eye.

- Pick-up tongs—These tongs have jaws that describe a series of curves, tapering to a point, that allow stock of different diameters to be gripped.

- Bolt tongs—These tongs have a bow in the center of the bit, terminating in a short, hollow bit. As the name suggests, they are particularly well suited to holding bolts and bolt-shaped objects.

## PUNCHES AND CHISELS

Punches and chisels are used to cut and shape stock, punch holes to mark, and otherwise decorate the surface of steel. A series of simple punch marks can transform a plain piece of work into a custom piece with all the charm and elegance of an antique. For the amount of beauty they add, punches and chisels are worth the time to make and use to decorate ironwork. They can still be found in hardware stores, but they are also simple to construct and are good practice for learning the art of working with medium-carbon steel, as well as annealing, hardening, tempering, and filing.

Holding chisels or punches over hot steel can be an uncomfortable proposition—you are in close proximity to a lot of heat. Long-handled chisels and punches help distance you from the worst of the heat, but it is a good idea to have a couple of tongs with jaws forged to securely grip these tools while you are working on hot steel. This will not only keep your hand clear of the heat and any misaimed blows striking your hand and fingers, but it also allows you to use shorter chisels and punches with a better transmission of the hammer force though the tool to your work.

### Chisels

Blacksmith chisels (fig. 28) are shaped, for the most part, like regular metalworking chisels. They are both designed to cut steel, but blacksmith chisels tend to have longer shafts to keep the smith's hand away from the hot iron.

### Punches

Punches come in a wide variety of shapes and answer to many uses (fig. 29). One of the handiest punches is the center punch. It is used to mark stock for forging, as well as to help drill bits to drill more precisely, serving as a guide for the bit to follow. Center punches are also used to create decorative patterning on steel and to carve and shape steel, such as eyes and nostrils on things like forged animal faces. Flat-faced punches are used to punch holes in stock and for various decorative applications.

Punches shaped as half rounds can be used to sink hemispheres, develop carvings, and countersink holes. Crescent-shaped punches can be used to develop leaf forms. Eye punches are flat-faced with a dimple in the center, put in with either a round-nosed punch or drilled into the annealed stock.

For cold work, the edge of these tools should be hardened and tempered to a reddish brown, with a blue running up the handle, to prevent it from chipping or deforming from hammer blows applied to the top of the tool's striking surface (more on tempering in chapter 5). If you are working only hot steel with your punches, the hardening and tempering are less critical, but it is still a good practice.

I have on occasion used thick-walled pipe cut to manageable length to answer the needs of an eye punch. I have also used it when working on hot stock or on softer materials like copper, which can be worked cold using punches of unhardened mild steel.

### Drifts

These punch-like tools are small pieces of stock, tapered on both ends (fig. 30). Their center section is the shape and desired cross section of a hole you wish to make in steel. First, punch a hole or use a slit chisel to make an opening in the steel; then, insert the

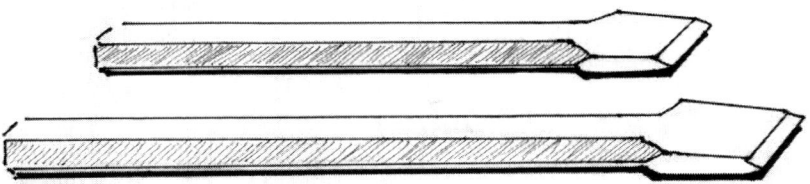

**Figure 28.** Blacksmith chisels.

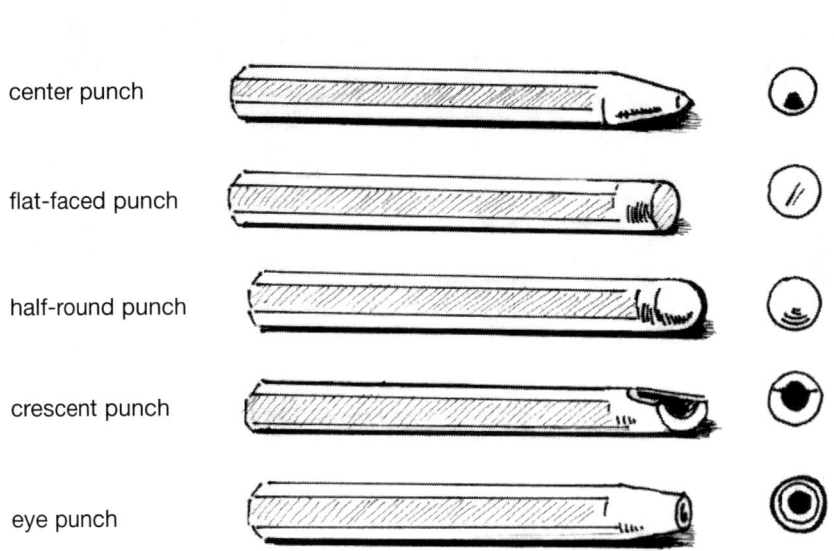

**Figure 29.** Punches.

# The Blacksmith's Tools

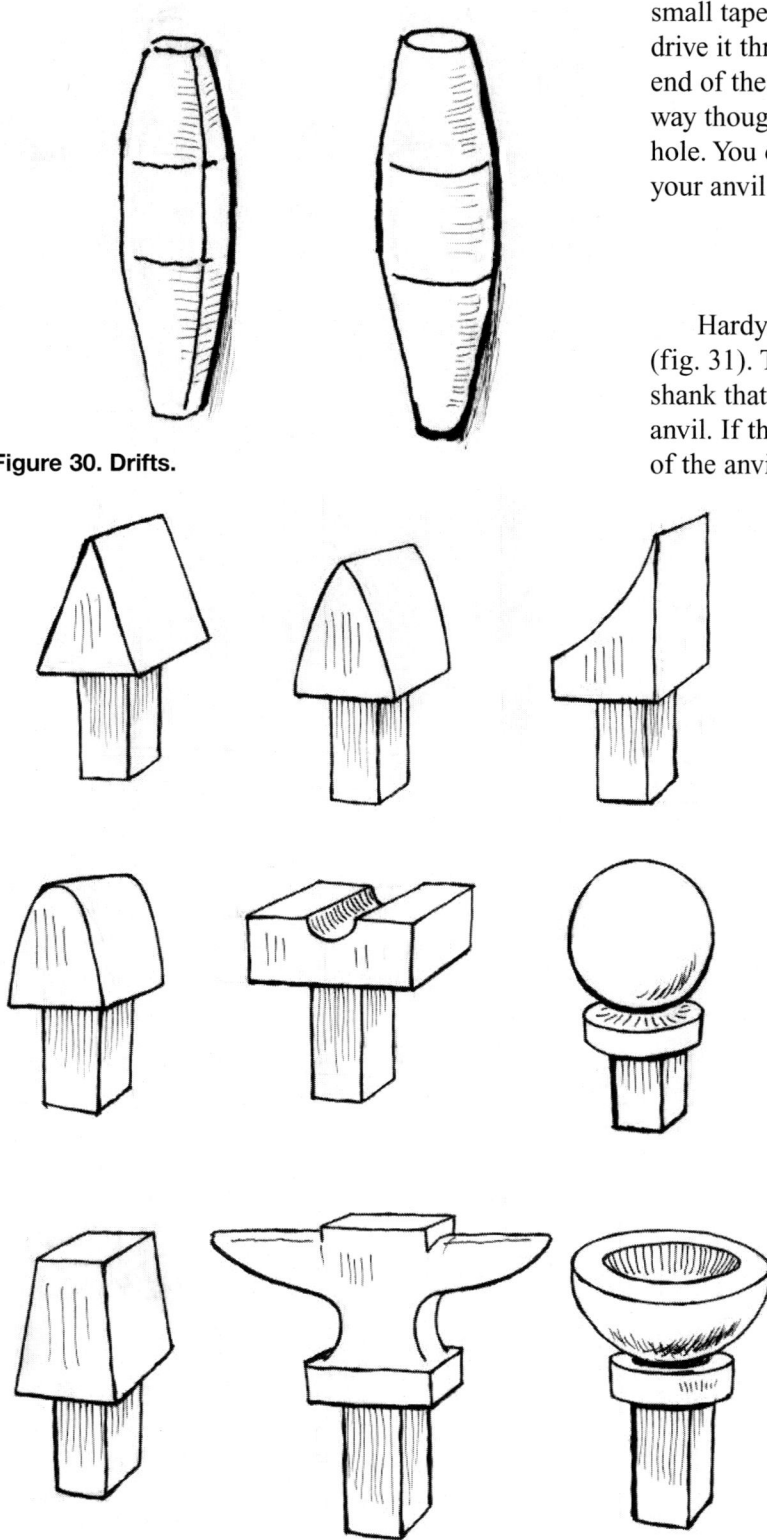

Figure 30. Drifts.

Figure 31. Hardy tools.

small tapered end of the tool into this cavity and drive it through the hot steel. The taper of the striking end of the tool allows the drift to be driven all the way though the hot steel without it binding in the hole. You can use a bolster block or the hardy hole of your anvil to punch through the stock.

## HARDY TOOLS

Hardy tools come in a wide variety of shapes (fig. 31). These tools have in common the square shank that should fit securely in the hardy hole of the anvil. If the shank protrudes a couple of inches clear of the anvil tail underneath, it greatly facilitates removal of this tool should it become stuck in the hole.

The most widely used and recognized is the hardy chisel, often simply referred to as the hardy. It is the short, stout chisel used to cut hot and cold steel stock. A thinner-bladed hardy chisel is used for cutting only hot stock. There are hardy tools with convex surfaces, a round top looking rather like a ball hitch, and concave shapes that allow forming hollow items like ladles and spoons. Hardy tools that look like miniature anvils offer the smith surface and tapered horns to form especially delicate work.

## HOLD-DOWNS

These days, many smiths work alone and do not always have the opportunity to employ the assistance of a striker. This is unfortunate, because without a striker it is much more difficult to take advantage of the full potential of the top and bottom tools used in blacksmithing.

In order to perform the three-handed task of holding stock, tool, and hammer, the lone smith needs a system to secure the stock in position to free his hands to hold the hammer and the tool to be struck, while keeping the hot steel securely in position for forging. A holdfast (fig. 32) can be made to fit into the hardy hole of the anvil and is simply bar stock the diameter of the tool hole, with a 90-degree bend that describes a small arc down to a flattened end. This tool is driven into the hardy hole and holds the work by simple friction.

Another expedient system employs a flexible steel cable, about the same size as bicycle cable, with a loop formed on both ends. Slip one loop through the hardy hole, pass stock through the top loop, and supply pressure to the bottom loop to hold the workpiece securely to the anvil face. This is done by putting your foot into the bottom loop and bearing down.

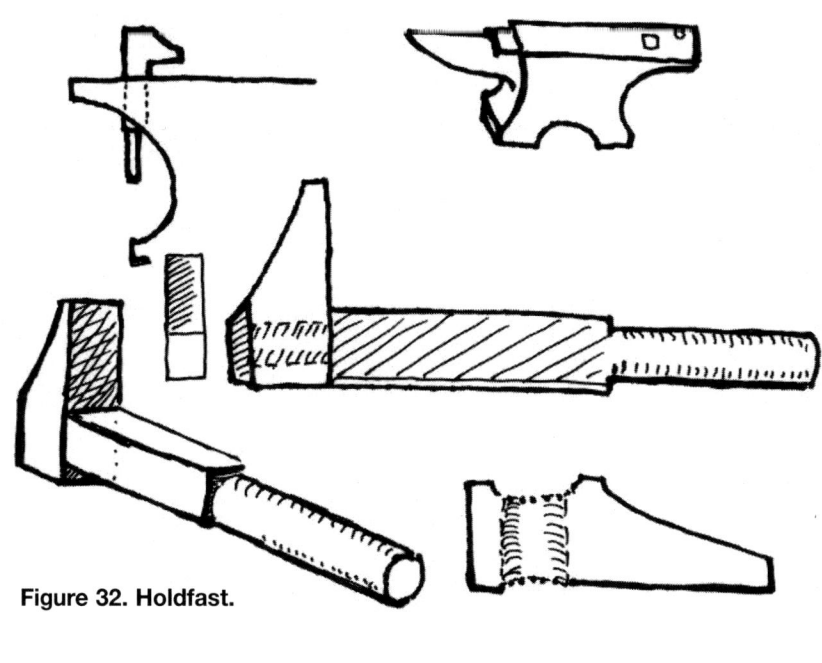

**Figure 32. Holdfast.**

## PUNCH PLATES AND CUTTING PLATES

Punch plates (fig. 33) augment the use of punches and chisels. They allow the ends of those tools to pass completely through the stock being worked (thus, by their use, preserving the anvil's working surface) while supporting the hot stock. A punch plate can be made of scrap stock between 3/16 to ½ inch thick, with enough mass to resist deforming with use. It will have round, square, or rectangular holes that match the diameter and shape of punches, chisels, and drifts. A punch plate allows the cutting tool to make a precise shearing cut rather than deforming the stock.

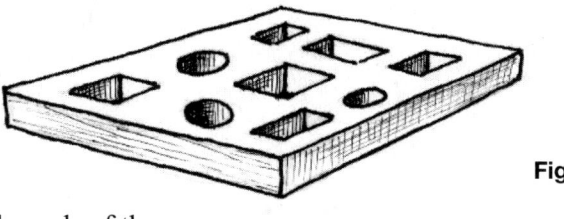

**Figure 33. Punch plate.**

Cutting plates (fig. 34) are simple flat plates of soft iron, copper, or aluminum and are usually bent on two sides to grip the sides of the anvil face, thus securing the plate to the anvil face to keep it from jumping or sliding off as stock is cut against it. Cutting plates also function to protect the surface of the anvil when doing work that might gouge its surface, such as angled cuts or glancing blows. They are by their nature expendable and can be made of lightweight stock. A cutting plate can also have a hardy attachment to secure it to the anvil (fig. 35).

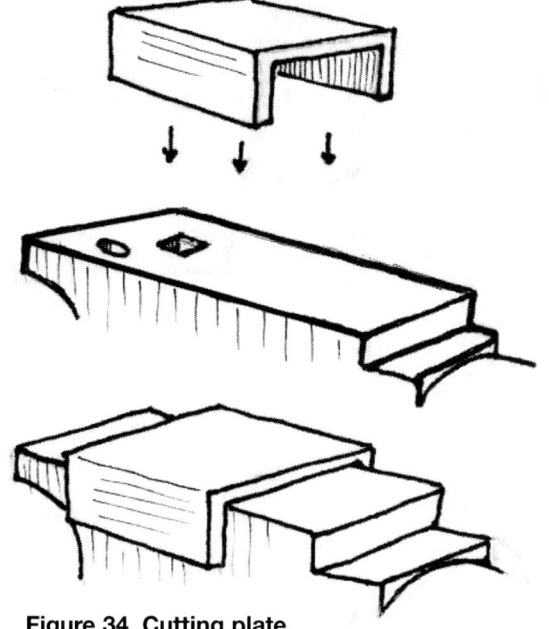

**Figure 34. Cutting plate.**

## The Blacksmith's Tools

### BOLSTER BLOCKS AND MONKEY TOOLS

These tools have holes pierced through them to allow stock to pass through so it can be upset (i.e., increased in diameter) farther up the piece (figs. 36–37). These are used to develop shoulders on tanged tools like wood chisels.

### Nail Headers

This is a simple bolster block on a handle long enough to be conveniently held by the smith (fig. 38). To use it, forge a nail to shape from stock that is slightly larger diameter than the finished nail shank will be. Forge the stock on the bar until it fits easily into the square hole of the header. Now, nick almost through the bar, leaving enough stock to form the head of the nail, and slip the hot nail into the header. Twist the stock free at the nick, set the nail header over the hardy hole with the nail shaft projecting out the bottom, and forge the head of the nail to shape on the header with a few well-placed blows. Quickly cool the nail and rap it free of the bolster block.

Figure 35. Cutting plate with hardy attachment.

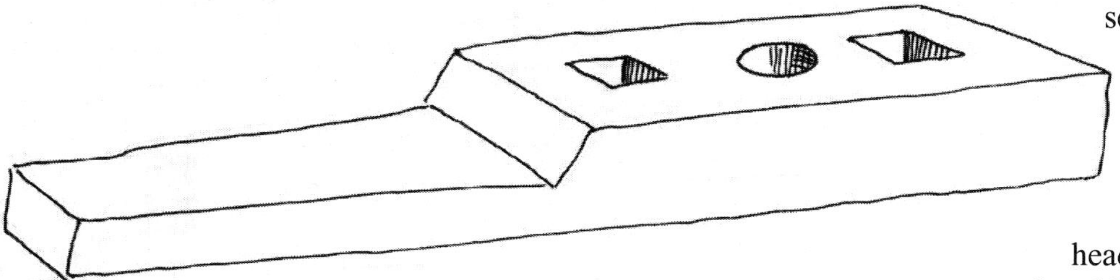

Figure 36. Bolster block.

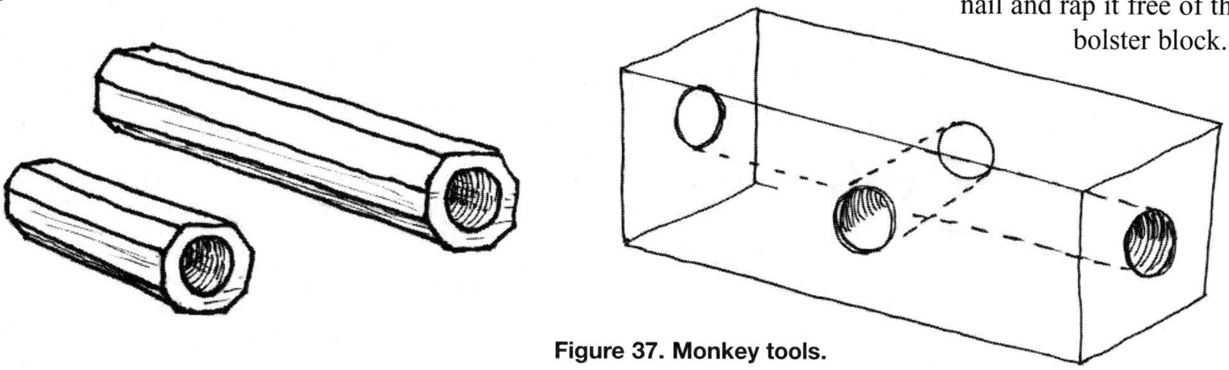

Figure 37. Monkey tools.

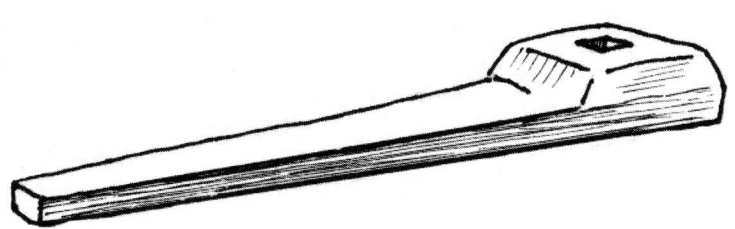

Figure 38. Nail header.

## SAWS

Hacksaws, band saws, and chop saws—each has its merits. For small work, a hacksaw may be your most appropriate tool, while a band saw or chop saw may be more suitable for larger work. Keep in mind that band saws and chop saws are faster, far more powerful, and extremely dangerous! Treat them with respect, and observe manufacturers' safety instructions and guidelines. You may think you can get away with a shortcut, but you might just get cut. When in doubt, don't!

### Hacksaws

These are saw frames equipped with an alloy steel blade that is used in conjunction with a vise to cut steel cold (fig. 39). They are useful where precise, thin cutting of cold material is required. The blades are replaceable and come in different tooth size and spacing, designated by teeth per inch (tpi). Therefore, a 24 tpi blade will have 24 teeth per inch of blade. This gives a fine cut and is used on thin stock, the general rule being that there should be at least two teeth in contact with the thickness of the stock being cut. Blades of 14 tpi cut faster and 10 tpi faster still. This is useful when cutting larger stock or softer material like copper, which tends to load up the teeth of a saw and make the blade cut less efficiently.

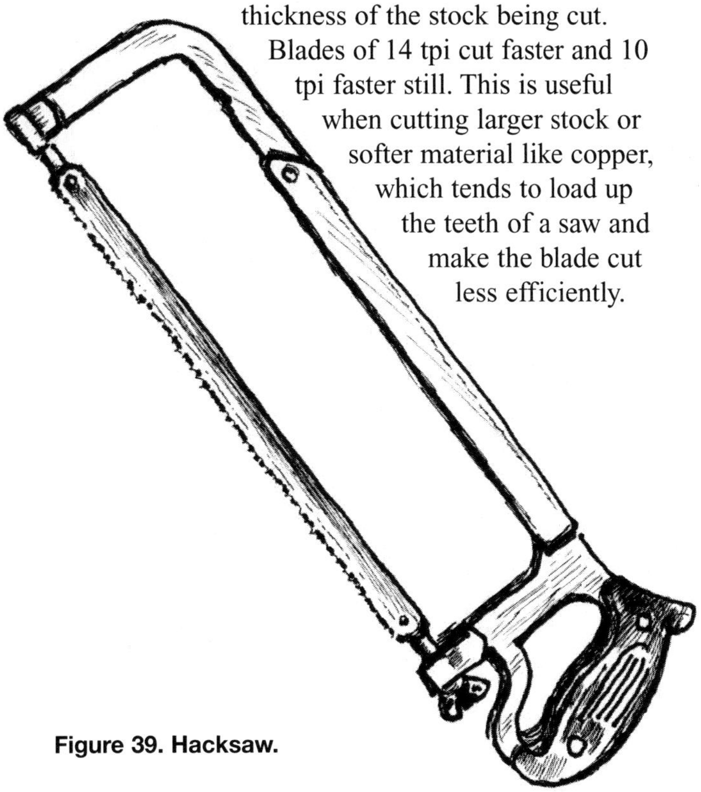

### Band Saws

Band saws (fig. 40) are machines that run a band of alloy steel with steel-cutting teeth, once again the size and spacing being designated by tpi. They have a system of pulleys that speed up or slow down the moving blade, with slower speeds being used to cut larger stock. Band saws allow you to use both hands to manipulate the stock. They cut low-carbon steel quickly and efficiently, as well as softer materials like nonferrous metal and wood.

Never get your fingers in the way of a band saw

Figure 39. Hacksaw.

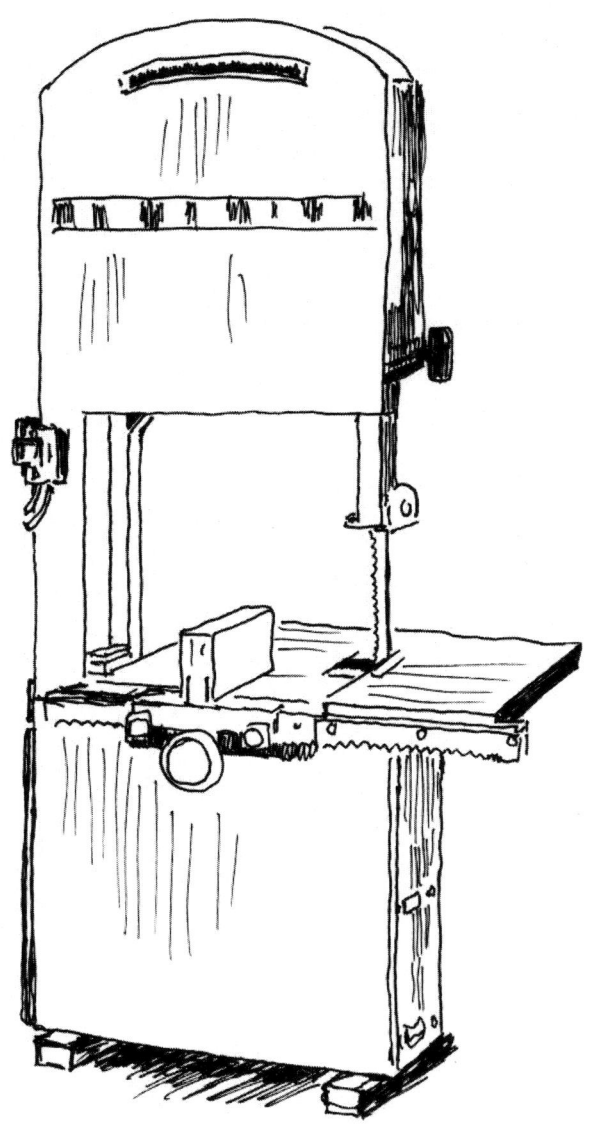

Figure 40. Band saw.

## The Blacksmith's Tools

blade. When cutting small stock, grip it with some tool. You can use a piece of wood to guide the piece as you cut it. *Do not* push a piece through with your hands. The blade can cut through suddenly and unexpectedly and send your fingers into its path. Band saws can cut through steel, so they will have no difficulty going through your fingers. These tools are famous for cutting off fingers, so stay clear. Band saws can also lose teeth suddenly, spitting them toward your face, so wear safety glasses.

### Chop Saws

The chop saw (also known as a cutoff, carbide, or abrasive saw) has a coarse grit meshed in a fibrous matrix to form its cutting blade (fig. 41). It is turned at great speed with lots of torque supplied by an attached motor. It looks a bit like a circular saw but is a stationary unit, the blade being lowered onto the work by a lever arm. The unit usually has an integral vise for securing the stock to be cut. These saws cannot be used to cut a radius; all cuts must be straight.

Chop saws use, in effect, very thin grinding wheels to grind very thin sections through steel. Hence, they make a grinding cut, showering sparks and carbide dust as the wheel wears down while cutting through the steel. They are capable of cutting through not only mild steel but also high-carbon steel quickly.

These saws cut through both hardened and unhardened steel and are indispensible when cutting sections of stock too big to anneal. Leaf springs from autos, coil springs, and steel cable (1080 improved plow) are all examples of material nearly impossible to cut cold without a chop saw.

These tools pose all the dangers of both a saw and a grinder, so keep your hands clear. They shower the operator with sparks and send particles of grit flying, so safety glasses are a must. A full face shield is recommended, as well as some means to avoid breathing the dust, which is abrasive and can eventually damage your lungs.

### WORK TABLES

Any heavy wood or steel table will serve as a workstation on which to assemble work or mount tools and machines (fig. 42). Make sure it is stable and has enough mass so it doesn't move about when you're working with power tools or at the vise. Good places to look for work tables include reuse centers, thrift shops, and yard sales. They are often available for very reasonable prices because they are large,

Figure 41. Chop saw.

Figure 42. Heavy work table.

heavy, ugly, or marred—just the thing for a blacksmith! Place the table away from the anvil and forge, as it is not used for hot metal and may be vulnerable to sparks.

## VISES

Every smith should have at least one small vise, but a larger vise is better. When it comes down to working on pieces that need to be filed or shaped with punches and chisels, the more mass the vise has, the better it will perform its function of holding your work secure and steady.

### Machinist's Vise

Machinist's vises (fig. 43) can be used in the blacksmith shop for holding stock that needs be worked hot or cold. This frees the smith's hands to use tools like chisels and punches while he applies hammer strokes to them.

Figure 43. Machinist's vise.

### Leg Vise

Also known as the blacksmith's vise, the leg vise (figs. 44–45) is forged from iron or steel and is a very robust tool, engineered to withstand the rough usage of the blacksmith's trade. The long leg of the vise serves to transmit the force from hammering down to the ground, thus saving wear and damage to the jaws and vise screw. Much precision work is extremely difficult, if not impossible, without this simple shop tool.

The blacksmith vise is around 40 inches from the top jaw to the bottom of the leg, and the jaws measure about 6 inches across. The unit is usually bolted to a heavy table or beam via the mounting plate. The bottom of the vise leg can be anchored and further stabilized by a large staple (not shown) that binds it to either the base of the beam or table leg to which it is mounted. The ferrule can act as a stabilizing rest in a hole in the floor or bottom support (e.g., steel plate, block of wood). Jaw tension is maintained by a simple leaf spring arrangement. The longer of the two jaws is stationary, and attached to it are the mounting bracket that holds the back plate clip and wedges, the tension spring, and a large bracket below it, which serves as a base for the vise

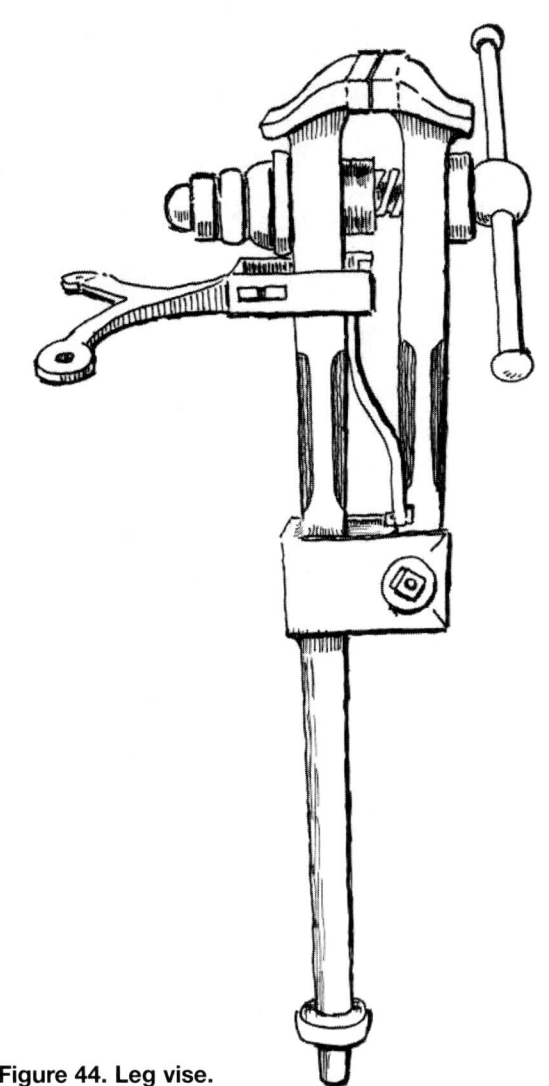

Figure 44. Leg vise.

## The Blacksmith's Tools

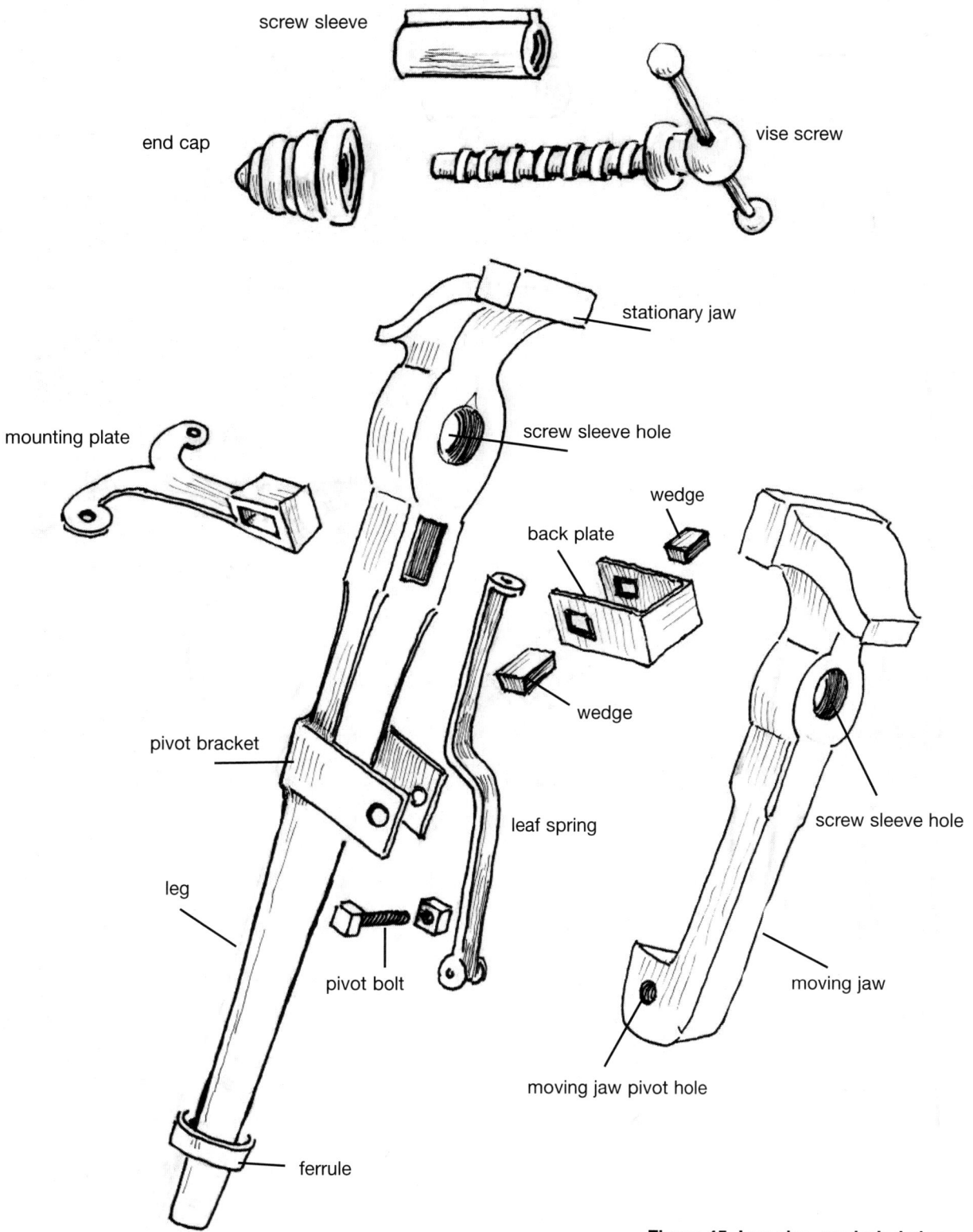

Figure 45. Leg vise, exploded view.

as well as the attachment pivot for the second, moving jaw. The large, coarse vise screw slides through receiving holes beneath each of the jaws and is locked in place by the end cap.

You can approximate the age of a leg vise by how ornate the end cap is. If I remember correctly, the rule of thumb is the older the vise, the more ornate the terminal screw cap. Leg vises you might come across for sale may be missing some components, but as long as both jaw sections are present and the screw and end cap are in good working order, other pieces can be replaced. If the vise is cheap enough, you may well consider buying it and then manufacturing parts to fit. Back plates, mounting brackets, and the tension spring are relatively easy to make. Over the years I have had the good fortune to come across about a half dozen leg vises missing these replaceable parts, at prices ranging from $10 to $50, compared to leg vises in good order running from $80 to $100 or more. Just beware: the screw needs to be inspected for wear damage. If the threads aren't in good shape, no amount of tightening will adequately secure them. The vise will not grip securely, and pieces can jump free of its grip.

The leg vise is best situated in close proximity to the forge and anvil so the smith can transfer work directly from the fire to it, lock it in place, and still have sufficient heat to work the piece. If your vise is too far from your heat source, it poses the same problem as when your anvil is placed too far from your forge: much of your working heat is wasted.

## SWAGE BLOCKS AND CONE MANDRELS

Swage blocks (fig. 46) are large cast-iron blocks usually weighing in excess of 100 pounds. Their surfaces are cast with a variety of hollow forms used to make ladles, bowls, spoons, and various agricultural forgings. The blocks often have square and round holes pierced through them, and all four sides usually have a series of grooves, from small and shallow to increasing gradations of depth and width, either half round or triangular. These are useful, for instance, if forging a series of wood-carving gouges.

The shape of the swage determines exactly what implement can be made with it, which is why a

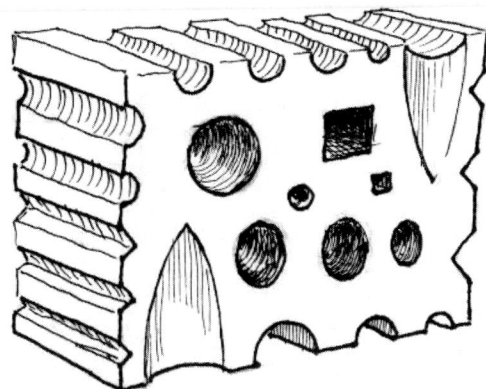

**Figure 46. Swage block.**

swage block can have such a variety of swages. The hot steel is pounded into the swage with a small hammer, making a concave spoon or ladle bowl, for instance. A top tool can have either a positive or negative contour, further determining the shape of the finished piece formed between the swage and tool. Swage blocks are often used with top tools to true up stock forged in round or square cross section. With the right swages and top tools, you can make round stock square and square stock round.

Cone mandrels look like a large cast-iron witch's hat (fig. 47). These tools are uncommon these days and, if I guess correctly, were mostly used in wagon making, being useful for forging bands and rings. They are exceedingly heavy and can be used like an anvil to forge stock and forge weld rings and bands on the tapered surface. There is usually a deep groove running up one side to accommodate the jaws of a pair of tongs holding the hot work.

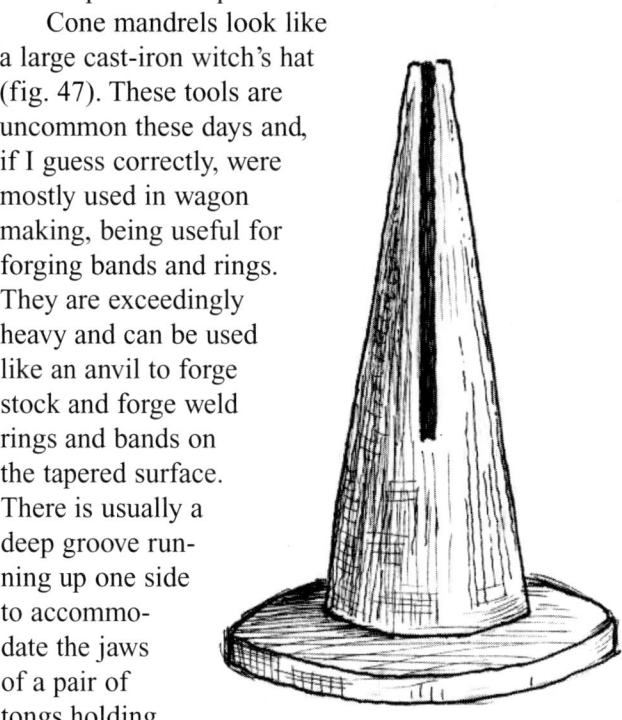

**Figure 47. Cone mandrel.**

## The Blacksmith's Tools

### FILES

Good files are a joy to work with—new files especially. Files of poor quality give poor results, require more effort, and are soon worn out. When storing good files, protect their cutting teeth. Some smiths store their files in canvas with pouches for each file, which can be rolled up to easily store or transport. Otherwise, you can simply wrap them in heavy paper, leather, or canvas.

File terminology (double cut, single cut, mill bastard, fine cut, etc.) designates the aggressiveness of the cutting action. They come in various lengths, from tiny needle files to files in excess of 2 feet, and in numerous cross sections, including flat, half round, square, knife edge, round, and rat-tailed (fig. 48). Good files have to be very hard to cut steel and consequently are very brittle. Do not hammer

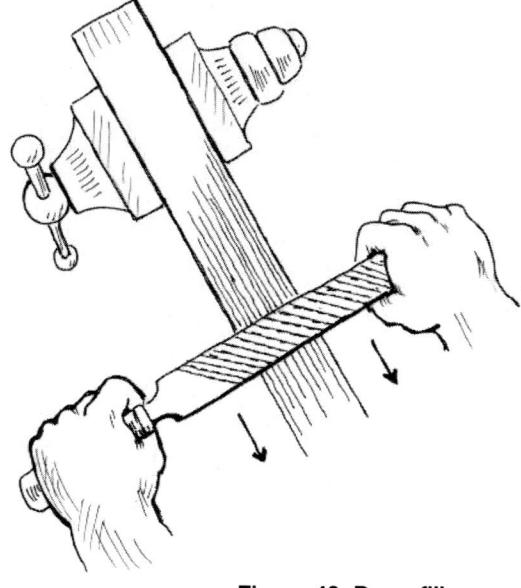

**Figure 49. Draw filing.**

them or try to bend or twist them. Even dropping one can break it.

Cutting with files takes some practice: use even, firm pressure; full strokes forward; and lift slightly for the return. You can also perform such tasks as draw filing, where you hold the file crosswise to the work, with one hand on top and the other on the handle, and stroke the length of the steel toward you in a smooth finishing action (fig. 49). This leaves an even surface, with all the cut marks lying in one direction. As this is most often done to impart a final finish surface to the steel, used files can be employed, which cut less aggressively and leave a smoother finish on the iron.

### WIRE BRUSHES AND WIRE WHEELS

A handheld wire brush with short, coarse bristles is an inexpensive and useful addition to your forge equipment (fig. 50). Scale, as noted earlier, is the oxide formed on hot iron and steel. It can interfere

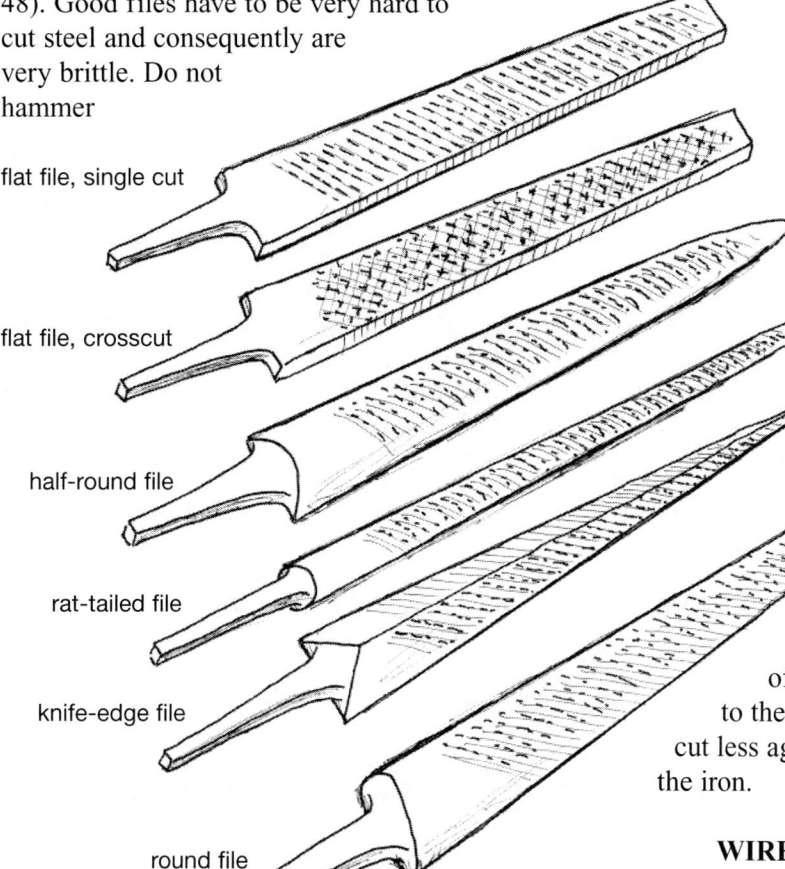

flat file, single cut

flat file, crosscut

half-round file

rat-tailed file

knife-edge file

round file

**Figure 48. Files.**

with forge welding, flake off and burn you as you work, and, when cool, suddenly pop off the work surface and jettison particles toward your eyes. But when the hot metal is removed from the fire, a quick pass with the wire brush will dislodge much of the scale. A good sharp rap of the hot steel on the anvil edge can accomplish this as well. Getting scale off hot iron will assist in later finishing work—the less scale you have on your work, the easier you will find it is to finish.

Once steel has cooled, scale still adhering to it shrinks tightly to the surface and is more difficult to remove. You might lock the piece in the vise to accommodate more aggressive use of the wire brush, or you can hit it with a wire wheel (fig. 51), which will remove fire scale quickly (a coarse wire wheel does the job best). A coarse Scotch-Brite wheel will also do the job of descaling admirably and has the added advantage of not throwing off broken bits of wire as you

**Figure 50. Wire brush.**

work. These bits will penetrate your clothing and are especially difficult to locate in wool and napped fibers. Obviously, the wires can penetrate you as well. Wearing denim makes it easier to locate the wire, and a face shield can help you avoid pulling wire out of your face later in the workday. Broken bits of wire will get into low-cut shoes, where they will lodge in your shoes and socks and torture you as they elusively resist all attempts at locating them.

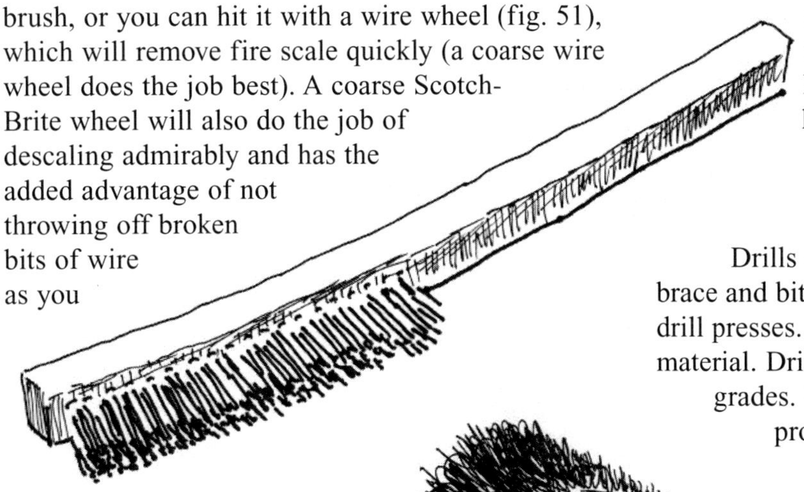

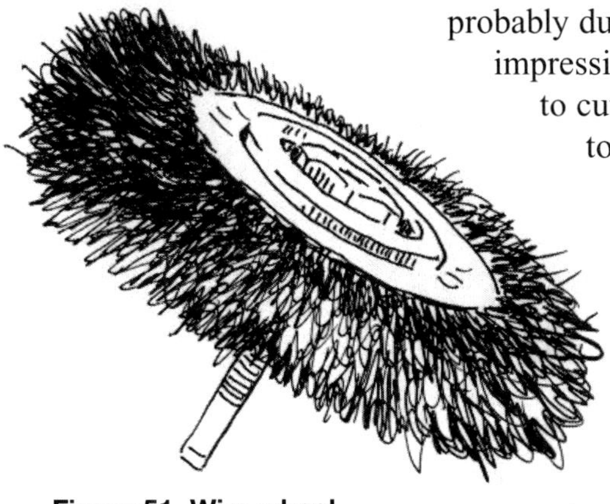

Wire wheels come in coarse, medium, and fine grades. A short metal shank protrudes from the wheel's center and allows it to be held securely by its power source, either a handheld drill or a bench-mounted apparatus. Besides descaling, wire wheels can be used to blend lines in work.

Keep your hands and fingers clear of the wire wheel—it can wear the flesh off your fingers with surprising speed. As when working with any high-speed rotary tool, secure any loose clothing or long hair. Wire wheels are very grabby, so stay alert when using one. Use a breakaway grip to keep from being dragged into the moving wheel if a piece you are working on gets caught. Unfortunately, wearing gloves while working with wire wheels greatly increases the risk of getting caught. Once again, it is a much safer option to resort to alternate methods like using Scotch-Brite wheels for descaling, which are less likely to grab the work or you.

## DRILLS

Drills can be manually operated, like the old brace and bit style, or power tools like hand drills or drill presses. They serve to cut precise holes in cold material. Drill bits come in wood- and metal-cutting grades. Using a wood-rated bit to cut steel will probably dull the bit without making much impression on the steel you are trying to cut. Bits come in sizes from tiny to extra large, with various alloy combinations available to cut metals without dulling the edges or being damaged by heat generated by friction.

Hand drills are portable and useful tools that allow you to bring the drill to the work rather than bring the work to the drill. This is especially handy when the workpiece is bulky or difficult to move.

Drill presses are machines with a drill attached to a table and a lever to lower the bit to the work (fig. 52). The pressure of the drilling cut is regulated by the pressure exerted on this lever by the operator.

**Figure 51. Wire wheel.**

## The Blacksmith's Tools

Drill presses, like band saws, usually have a series of reduction pulleys that regulate the speed at which the bit turns. Adding a few drops of oil or other suitable lubricant to the surface being drilled will greatly reduce friction and the accompanying heat it generates. This simple expedient will help save your bits from the rapid wearing that occurs after the bit has been annealed (softened) by heat. Running the bits at slower rotation also helps decrease the heat caused by friction.

Drill bits can be secured in the drill press either by means of a collet, which is tightened around the bit, or by a chuck and chuck key arrangement. If your drill uses the latter, be especially careful to always remove the chuck key before you begin drilling. Besides damaging the drill, it could fly out and damage you.

Use a drill press vise to hold small work when drilling; lacking this, use vise grips to hold small work. When work has sharp edges, you will most especially want to have it locked in vise grips. When the bit breaks through, there is a tendency for it to grab the piece and spin it with great force. It can cut the daylights out of you.

### GRINDERS AND BUFFERS

While a hand file and a sharpening stone can be used to shape and put a final edge on your work, you'll soon find that it's hard and time-consuming work. Grinders and buffers do the job faster and better. But caution is advised: a moment's inattention can remove far too much stock, not to mention parts of your hide. Pay particular attention and be on your guard when working with any power equipment in your shop.

#### Bench Grinders

A bench grinder (fig. 53) is a motor with an arbor on one or both ends to which are attached composite stone wheels of various grit. These stone wheels can be very coarse, cutting steel quickly but leaving a rough surface. Finer-grit wheels remove stock less quickly but leave a finer surface on the

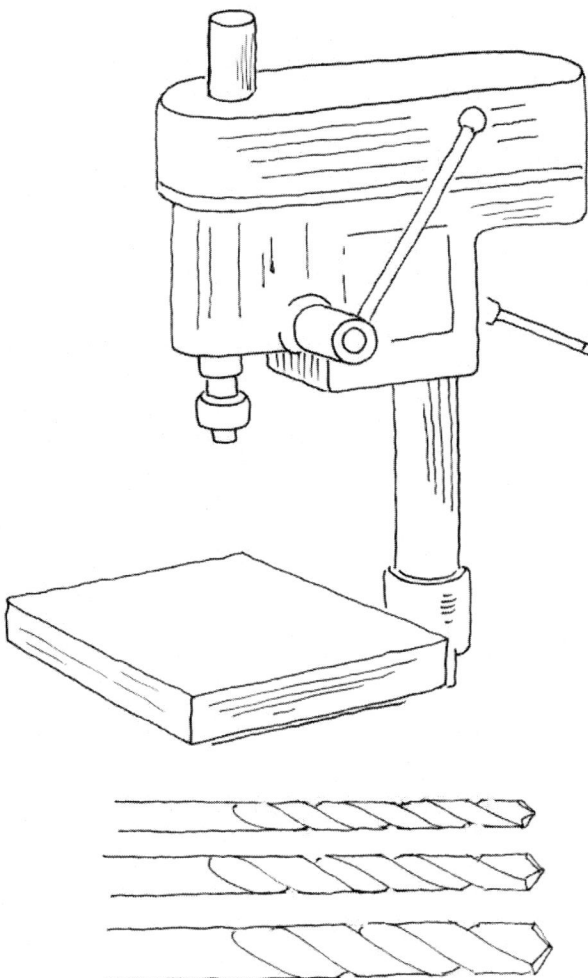

Figure 52. Drill press and drill bits.

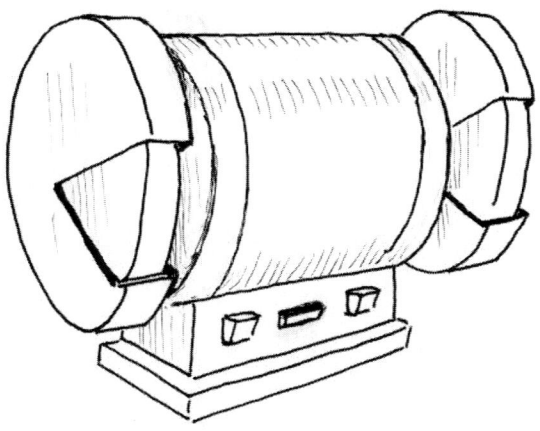

Figure 53. Bench grinder.

work. They are employed to shape stock and grind edges on various tools. As I make a lot of edged tools, the grinders in my shop see a lot of use.

Whenever you grind anything, you will produce a lot of dust, and this will find its way into your lungs. Don't think you do not need to take precautions because you are only doing a little grinding—every day of exposure adds up. When grinding, wear a respirator or at least a dust mask. Using a full face shield is advisable, and safety glasses are a must due to sparks and particles thrown from the grinding.

### Belt Grinders

Also called belt sanders, these employ a belt of reinforced paper, cloth, or fiber that is impregnated on one side with grit (fig. 54). These belts cut quickly, without heating stock as quickly as a grinding wheel. The belts come in a variety of cutting grits and allow you to grind stock through a series of finer and finer grits until you can attain a mirror finish. This tool is nearly indispensible for anyone wishing to produce knives and edged tools.

Aside from the hazard posed from accidently grinding off your fingerprints on the face of the belt, you also must beware of the side of the belt, which is a very thin, strong edge moving at great speed. Avoid getting your fingers near this, as it cuts deep and fast—a really nasty paper cut.

As with bench grinders, belt sanders produce a lot of dust and sparks. Wear appropriate safety gear. Respirators are even more important to use with these tools, as the grits can be very fine, and some of the materials you grind can produce an irritating and sometimes even toxic dust. Items that come to mind include antler, horn, bone, shell, composites, plastics, and some exotic hardwoods.

### Buffers

A buffer is like a bench grinder, but instead of stone wheels, it employs stitched fibers like cotton cloth in a variety of sizes and thicknesses (fig. 55).

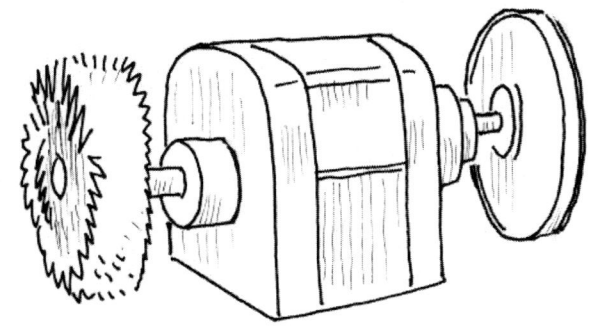

**Figure 55. Buffer.**

The buffing wheel's action comes from a fine cutting compound in a grease or wax base that's applied against the moving wheel to charge its surface. Buffing wheels are used to blend lines and to achieve anything from a satin finish to a bright mirror polish on work. They are usually employed in the last stages of finishing work.

Buffing wheels, like wire wheels, can be grabby, so use a breakaway grip when working. The buffing wheel is especially dangerous in that it can grab workpieces and fling them back at you with great speed and force. Wear a face shield and heavy leather apron. As with the grinders, the dust generated is cumulative, so protect your lungs and avoid breathing the dust.

## TORCHES AND RELATED TOOLS

Small propane torches have a number of uses

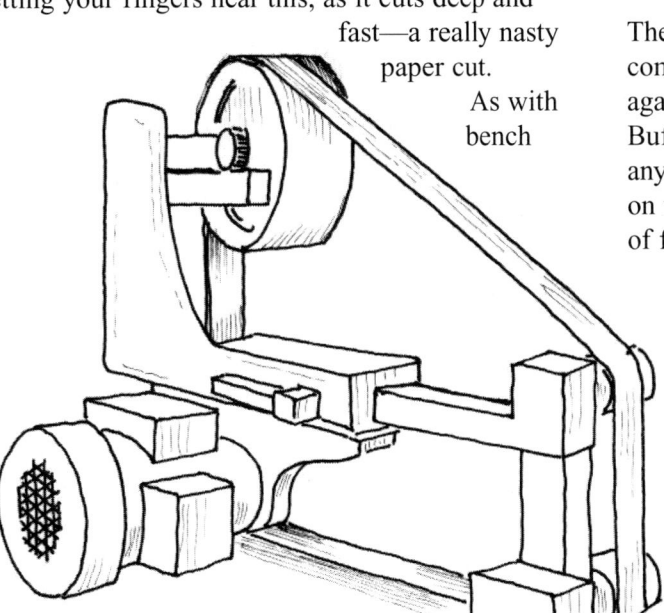

**Figure 54. Belt grinder.**

# The Blacksmith's Tools

in the forge, including starting the fire, tempering, soldering, and heating small work. Self-lighting torches are especially convenient.

I do not make frequent use of the following tools, but every blacksmith should be aware of their potential in the shop. Refer to other sources for more detailed descriptions of these tools and how to best employ them.

- Oxyacetylene torch—Oxygen acetylene torches are useful for such tasks as gas welding, brazing, cutting steel, and localized heating.

- Arc welder—Metal inert gas welding (MIG), tungsten inert gas welding (TIG), and other shielded gas welders use a gas to protect the weld electrode from atmospheric oxygen, giving a smoother weld bead.

- Electric welder—These are especially useful when assembling iron work such as gates, where welding in the forge would be impracticable.

- Plasma torch—These torches cut sheet steel like no other tool. Complex outlines that would be difficult to cut with saws and chisels are cut out with ease using a plasma torch.

## QUENCH TUBS

Quench tubs can be made from barrels, half barrels, wine/whisky barrels, 50-gallon steel drums, half drums, sturdy plastic pails, or any similar vessel large enough to accommodate your work. It is a good idea to have more than one container for water in the blacksmith shop. A wooden barrel cut in half makes an interesting container, but they tend to leak and are heavy even when empty. Fifty-gallon steel drums are lighter but tend to rust out eventually. Plastic is light and rust resistant, but you must be careful not to melt or pierce it.

For oil quenching, the container must be fireproof (e.g., steel can, ceramic tub). Oil quenches tend to flash, and this could easily become a dangerous situation if the container were to melt, break, or catch on fire, as it would then spew flaming oil onto your shop floor—a real potential disaster scenario. (More on quenching in chapter 5.)

# CHAPTER 4

# Materials

When you are just starting in blacksmithing or are new to an area, you need to find sources for coal, propane, tools, steel, and various supplies. The phone book is, not surprisingly, a good place to start. Look under welding supplies, farrier supplies, fuel, steel, and salvage and junk yards, to name a few. The Internet is also a great source for information, from the many blacksmithing organizations to resources like Craigslist. It is well worth searching online to see what is out there.

If you are fortunate enough to have a local chapter of a blacksmith organization in your area, it might prove the best resource of all. There are several organizations geared toward blacksmithing these days, and one group that comes to mind is the Artist Blacksmith Association of North America (ABANA). This organization has chapters all over the world.

## BUYING TOOLS

Sometimes you just get lucky. You stop on a long car drive to investigate a sign for a flea market, and it's a huge tumble of barns and buildings, literally stacked floor to ceiling with various antiques, antiques-to-be, and all sorts of unidentifiables. Around the outside walls are mounds of rusting objects, ancient agricultural machines and implements, rolls of wire, fence sections—and blacksmith tools! Railroad forges, rivet forges, leg vises, swage blocks, hammers, tongs, and anvils everywhere, from small to massive! It sounds like a dream for most blacksmiths—but it happened to me! It was in a small rural community in coastal Maine. The prices were good. Needless to say, I left there considerably poorer but very happy.

The point here is that looking for used blacksmithing equipment these days can be a matter of pure luck, and it pays to keep your eyes open. Such places as farrier supply houses sell all the new blacksmith tools and fixtures you could desire, but the prices are very dear. When looking to put together the basic tools for blacksmithing, it is hard to beat the networking and resource potential of organizations like ABANA. Not only is it a way to contact sellers of used tools and likeminded people interested in the craft, but it is also a remarkably dedicated teaching organization.

## FINDING FORGEABLE STOCK

When it comes to steel, commercial supply houses have the advantage of selling new stock in specific composition, lengths, and dimensions. You know what you are getting, as opposed to relying on scrap of unknown origin.

Don't overlook specialty outlets for specific types of stock. Welding supply shops, for example, carry brazing rods of various diameters. It is referred to as bare bronze, and it can be hot formed. It also serves as pin stock and, of course, as brazing stock.

These days there are a lot of choices in the basic product available to the ironworker.

### Iron

Wrought iron has little to no carbon and does not harden. It has a fibrous grain due to its silica content and forms a patina as it weathers that serves to protect it from further degradation from the elements. As wrought iron is much less likely to be available to the smith, the word "iron" is often used to indicate mild steel.

### Mild Steel

Low-carbon, or mild, steel is steel that has about 18 to 20 points of carbon content and forges more or less like iron, being relatively easy to shape, able to withstand high heat, and not being hardenable. Mild steel is offered in two types from steel supply houses: hot rolled and cold rolled. Hot-rolled stock comes in 20-foot lengths and has fire scale adhering to the surface. It is less expensive than cold-rolled steel. Cold-rolled steel is hot-rolled steel that has undergone an extra rolling process that removes the scale, forms more precise diameter stock, and work hardens the surface, making it slightly more brittle than hot-rolled stock. It comes in 12-foot sections and is more expensive than hot-rolled stock of comparable diameter.

### Spring Steel

Medium-carbon steel is also known as spring steel. Springs and tools that need to withstand shock and deflection are best made from medium-carbon steel. Automobile leaf and coil springs are usually made from 5160, which is a medium-carbon steel containing 60 points of carbon with a couple other trace elements in the mix. Scrap car springs can serve the blacksmith as an inexpensive source of this useful steel. It is best hardened in thin oil, such as a vegetable oil. Quenching this steel in water may crack it.

### Alloy Steel

Modern high-carbon steels come in a staggering variety of alloys, each answering to a specific application and each having special instructions for heating, forging, annealing, hardening, and tempering. Numerous combinations of vanadium, tungsten, cobalt, manganese, nickel, chromium, and other elements will all impart specific characteristics to alloy steels.

Stainless steel is an alloy of steel and chromium (and sometimes another element, such as nickel or molybdenum). While forgeable, it is full of tricks, including fairly exotic hardening and tempering requirements, so we won't be dealing with it here.

### Basic Steel

On to the simple, straightforward, stable steels—steels like W1, W2, O1, 1095, 1080, 1060, 1020, and 1018.

W1 and W2 are high-carbon steels that are hardened by water quench. They are used for things like files and bits for jackhammers.

O1 and the 10 series are oil-hardening steels. 1095 is nearly as high carbon as O1, having 95 points of carbon. 1080 has 80 points of carbon and is often employed for wire cable. 1060, with 60 points of carbon steel, is also known as medium-carbon steel or spring steel and is found, as noted above, in such applications as vehicle leaf and coil springs. 1020 has 20 points of carbon and does not harden; it is referred to as structural steel, iron, low-carbon steel, or mild steel. 1018 has 18 points of carbon and is not as common as 1020. It is useful for any work requiring great ductility.

# Materials

## SCROUNGING STOCK

Salvage yards can serve as a source of inexpensive stock for the blacksmith. Keep in mind how much stock of similar diameter would cost per foot from a steel supplier. You rather defeat your purpose if you are paying new stock prices for old, and when buying from a steel supplier, you know what you are getting. Scouting a salvage yard takes some skill to find what you want.

One problem with gathering material from a yard is trying to figure out what you are looking at. Some yards employ knowledgeable staff who can tell you what is what, but it never hurts to check. There are a few methods you can employ to help you determine the composition of the metal you are looking at.

### Magnetism

A small magnet is the first of your diagnostic tools—this is how you can separate ferric from nonferrous materials. Iron, steel, cast iron, nickel, and some stainless steels are all magnetically responsive. Nonferrous materials like aluminum, copper, brass, and bronze are nonmagnetic.

### Rust

The nonferrous materials don't rust like iron and steel; instead, as they oxidize, they develop a surface patina that often masks the true color of the metal beneath. A small coarse file will help you quickly penetrate the surface to see what is below, copper being reddish, brass golden, and bronze a darker greenish gold. Bronze is also going to be harder to file, with brass next and copper softest.

With iron and steel, it is not so easy to determine what you have. Rust is actually an indicator of sorts. Wrought iron will tend to show striations in the material, which has almost a wood grain appearance. Steel will usually pit as it rusts.

### Carbon Content

It is a little trickier to determine if the steel is low or high carbon. The best way I have found to determine the general nature and carbon content of scrap steel is to rely on the old form-and-function rule. Car springs, both leaf and coil, are generally 5160 steel. This is a good medium-carbon steel; it is very stable and makes excellent punches and chisels. It can be forged into edged tools and is a tough, resilient material. It is an oil-hardening steel and will likely crack if it is heated and then cooled in water.

Architectural iron, if it is very old, such as fence sections from a graveyard, could very well be wrought iron. Outdoor fences were some of the last widespread uses of wrought iron in this country, still being used into the 1950s. More likely, fence sections found in a salvage yard will be mild steel. Either way, you're not going to see carbon of any great content in such applications.

Old files, as well as things like old jackhammer bits and chisels, tend to be W1 or W2 steel. Steel cables tend to be 80-point carbon steel and are a devil to cut sections from in a yard. They also deteriorate with rust and are sometimes galvanized, which makes them less desirable for forging.

Black pipe is going to be very low-carbon steel. Once again, avoid pipe that is galvanized.

Cast iron is not a suitable material for forging—it cracks and crumbles. Scrap cast iron, like forge fire pots, are certainly useful to a smith, but they are brittle, and most examples you might find in a scrap yard are going to be broken. Cast iron is not readily welded by any means that I know of.

Flat stock in 20-foot lengths is generally mild steel. If it happens to be medium or high carbon and priced below market for mild steel, it is worth buying either way. Twelve-foot sections of stock tend to be cold-rolled mild steel and have sharper edges than hot-rolled stock.

A common way to determine a steel's carbon contest is to perform a spark test, which works by grinding on known stock, like a piece of mild steel or an old file, and comparing the shape and size of the spark to the spark created by the unknown material. The larger and more explosive (sparkler-like) a spark, the more carbon it has. A file will throw a shower of sparks not unlike a Fourth of July sparkler. (Carbon burns with a white light, so the more carbon the brighter the spark.) Lower carbon throws smaller and cooler, more reddish sparks. The problem I have encountered with this test is that some alloy steels of high carbon content do not spark anywhere near as much as their carbon content should warrant, some even throwing small, reddish sparks.

A much more reliable test is to heat the stock till it is nonmagnetic (this is the critical heat at which the steel will first harden), quench in water, and then test it with a file. If the file skates off the steel without biting—surprise!—it is high-carbon steel. See what happens with another small test piece in an oil quench. If it cracks in the water bath but not in the oil, then it is likely an oil-hardening steel.

# CHAPTER 5

# Basic Blacksmithing
## The Essentials

You've got your forge, your tools, adequate fuel, good ventilation, the proper clothing, and a healthy respect for shop safety. Now what? You'll need a project, of course, something simple that won't daunt or overtire you.

Before starting on your project, take the time to read through this chapter. Practice the various shaping techniques using stiff clay to model bends, twists, and scrolls. The clay will deform and move in much the same way as hot iron without the added dangers associated with working with incandescent metal. Then begin by just getting a feel for the heat you need and how the hammer is used. Understand how the metal changes as it cools. Practice each shaping technique in isolation before making it a crucial part of a finished product.

### SELECTING STOCK

When selecting stock, choose material that will give you the best results for the project you wish to make. Try to select material that is close to the finished diameter of your end product, thus relieving you of needless heating and hammering and saving your energy as you work.

Take into account the use your end product will be put to and choose accordingly the carbon content you will need to facilitate this. If you are forging nails, then you will want low-carbon steel—i.e., material strong enough to penetrate wood, but with the ability to be bent or clinched over. A center punch, by contrast, must mark and penetrate steel without deforming its point. Its handle must be able to withstand the force of hammer blows without bending or being so brittle as to chip when struck. The ideal material for such tools is medium-carbon steel, 60-point carbon content, hardened in oil and tempered to a reddish brown at the tip and a blue for the handle.

For razors and tools that will cut and keep a keen edge, high-carbon steel like O1 is a good choice. It is an oil-hardening steel, and if the edge is left a deep yellow, it will hold an edge quite a long time. Temper back from the edge to a deep blue to impart flexibility to the tool and afford it some measure of resistance to breaking. We will discuss tempering further later in this chapter.

## BUILDING AND MAINTAINING A FIRE

Your fire is a constantly changing environment. You start out with your green fuel, soft coal for instance. You ignite this with a smaller fire of kindling. As you burn off the impurities in the coal, it begins to puff up into what is known as coke. This is your real fuel. Soft coal before it has coked up gives a poor heat—it is a greasy, smoky, dirty fire until it has had a chance to become coke. Putting steel into green coal will not heat the material adequately and is injurious to the metal due to impurities in the coal, sulfur being the main villain in this case. Build your fire to the point where you have a good bed of glowing coal beneath and above the steel you wish to heat. Keep the fire fed by adding green coal to the edges, allowing it to coke up before dragging it into the fire as the older fuel is consumed. From time to time, you might thrust a thin poker into the base of the fire to keep the air blast free to reach the coal above.

A blacksmith strives to maintain a reducing fire. A reducing fire is one that consumes the oxygen that is present, thereby reducing the amount of free oxygen available to react with the hot metal in the fire. An oxidizing fire has an excess of oxygen; this unconsumed oxygen is then available to chemically react with the hot iron, producing the ferric oxide known as fire scale. Fire scale, as described earlier, is brittle and dangerous to hammer. It also mars the work and is a barrier to welding.

A reducing fire is made from a compact bed of coke closely surrounded by coal. The heat is reflected inward by the coke, and the available oxygen within this closed type of fire is rapidly used up—that is, reduced. Remember that the source of oxygen is from the bottom of the forge, so if fuel at the bottom is allowed to become exhausted, more air from the blower reaches your iron stock. In order to maintain a reducing fire, the blacksmith must add fuel regularly to the bottom of the fire.

As you work, impurities in the fuel will begin to coalesce at the bottom of your fire. This becomes a crude, glass-like substance called a clinker. As it gathers in the bottom of the forge, it will begin to block the airflow to your fuel, and as you work you will notice the steel heating slower and less evenly. When this occurs, discontinue the blast and reach into the bottom of the fire with your poker. You can sometimes hook the hot clinker with the poker and pull it out in one piece. This will clear the block to your airflow and you can continue working. Sometimes the clinker just breaks apart, and while the airflow is restored for a brief while, the clinker that isn't removed will recoalesce in the bottom of your fire pot, once again blocking your air. Clinkers can stick to the hot steel you are working on and can also form hot pockets that will heat the steel unevenly or, worse, act like a blowtorch, burning the steel in one place while leaving adjacent areas nearly cold.

### Coal

Soft coal, hard coal, coke, and charcoal can all be used in blacksmithing. Charcoal was a popular fuel in 19th-century America. Coke is an ideal fuel, as it produces even heat with little or no smoke. Bituminous coal is readily converted to coke during combustion. Anthracite is a hot, long-burning fuel and is used when a hot, clean fire is desired. The choice is sometimes dictated by price or availability, but any or all of these fuels will provide a fire that is hot enough to heat metal to forging temperature. If money and availability is no object, experiment and choose the fuel that works best for you.

### *Soft Coal*

Soft coal, bituminous coal, comes in various sizes: stoker, nut, and pea coal, sometimes referred to as blacksmith or farrier coal. The names give a good idea of the approximate size of the coal lumps. Larger pieces can be easily broken up with a hammer.

Soft coal has been, in my experience, the best overall fuel for blacksmithing. When it is heated, it burns off the majority of impurities and becomes coke. The coke is mostly composed of carbon; as noted, it forms a light, spongy mass, kind of like black Styrofoam but a bit heavier. Coke is coal that has had time to burn off its thick, oily, black smoke and unwanted components like sulfur (that is what gives burning soft coal part of its characteristic bouquet). This thick, oily, sulfur-charged air also accounts for the rapid rusting of iron stovepipe when it is employed as part of the forge hood stack.

## *Coke*

Coke, precooked coal, is available in some locations. It is a little more expensive than raw coal, but pound for pound you are not paying for the extra dross weight of the various elements that you would have to burn off anyway. This product is also known as industrial coke, or breeze.

## *Hard Coal*

Hard coal, anthracite coal, is coal that has spent a longer time in the earth. It tends to break into square fractures and usually has less sulfur content than soft coal. It is most commonly used for heating homes equipped with coal-burning stoves. Although it is a cleaner-burning fuel, hard coal doesn't actually coke up—instead, it turns to ash as it burns. This ash settles to the bottom of the fire pot, where it quickly collects in such density that it occludes the air blast from your blower, making the fire gradually, but inexorably, lose its heat potential. The hard coal fire thus tends to quickly self-extinguish in the forge. This makes for a difficult fire to tend, one you must constantly clear of ash as you work. Some smiths swear by hard coal, but I mostly swear at it.

## *Charcoal*

Charcoal, not a coal per se, is usually produced from hardwoods such as oak and hickory. The wood is burned in an environment that allows only enough air to cook off most of the water and volatile elements from the wood, leaving the carbon. This incomplete combustion leaves behind light chunks of charcoal that is an excellent forge fuel. It provides good heat and is free of sulfur, which all coal seems to have to a lesser or greater degree. Charcoal, then, is the fuel of choice when a really clean fire is desired or required.

The disadvantage of charcoal is the speed with which it is consumed in the forge fire. With coal lasting perhaps twice as long pound for pound, charcoal is relatively expensive as a fuel source. The fact that charcoal is a lightweight fuel must also be taken into account, as an overzealous blast of air can blow the fire right out of the forge. When the air blast is applied, charcoal produces what in earlier times were known as gledes. These are the floating sparks that the children try to catch in the poem by Henry Wadsworth Longfellow, *The Village Blacksmith*. These sparks are not so hot and vicious as those thrown from a hot piece of steel, and they extinguish on the way to the ground. If you are working a charcoal fire and require a robust blast of air, lay a board of oak on top of the fire; its weight will keep the charcoal from being blown out of the fire pot.

## The Gas Forge

Gas forges are easy to use and set up and are more and more common. Their fuel source is widely available, propane tanks being sold at most hardware stores. The interior of a gas forge is made of firebrick and/or refractory clay.

One of the main attractions of the gas forge is its ease of use. You crack a tank valve, hit a spark button, and your forge is lit. Fine-tuning the heat of your fire and the speed at which you consume your fuel is achieved by adjusting a regulator knob (fig. 56). By being able to adjust to specific heat ranges, you can work several irons in the fire with little danger of burning them. For production work, the gas forge is easily the most effective option.

Cranking the pressure to about 20 lbs. psi will be

**Figure 56. Propane gas regulator.**

likely as high as you need to go with a gas forge. You will eventually heat the firebrick until it is incandescent, at which time you will be able to weld medium-carbon steel. Low-carbon steel is a little more difficult to weld in a gas forge, as it needs just a bit more heat than the higher carbon steels. This can be remedied by adding a blower to supply a forced blast of air to the fire, which will greatly increase the heat potential of your gas forge.

The biggest drawback of many commercial propane forges is that it is hard to achieve welding heat in one. The fire tends to be an oxidizing fire. By comparison, a smith using a coal forge can produce an oxidizing fire or a reducing fire by placement of his fuel.

Some firebrick linings are adversely affected by welding fluxes such as borax, which eats away at the brick like acid. Flux also fuses to the firebrick at the bottom of the forge. This becomes an oozy mass when the firebrick heats up and tends to glue itself to hot metal laid upon it. A sacrificial plate of stainless steel sheet will serve as a barrier between the accumulating flux and the firebrick.

When heating nonferrous material for forging, it is especially wise to use such a plate in the bottom of the gas forge in case your material should melt while it is being heated. The plate will catch the molten metal and facilitate its removal.

A good example of why you should do this occurred to me when I accidentally melted the end of a copper bar in a gas forge. I had been welding steel the day before and, having not taken the precaution of inserting a catch plate, I had accumulated a thick pool of flux in the bottom. Some of the molten copper fused into this pool of flux. The upshot was that the next day, as I was attempting to forge weld out of the fire, nothing would stick. After several welds failed, I examined the steel closely and found each item had a thin coating of copper on it. The copper had boiled out of the flux and formed a vapor in the hot forge, which had literally copperplated everything that went into the fire. Once I had laboriously removed the dense layer of molten flux, I was once again able to forge weld. I now use a stainless plate to make cleanup easier.

## BASIC SMITHING: GETTING STARTED

Take a bar of steel—a good size to start out on is ½-inch square stock, mild steel, hot rolled. This size will hold the heat longer than smaller stock, giving you more time at the anvil for forging, while not being too large to be able to forge it with relative ease. If you choose a length of bar from 2 to 3 feet, you will probably be able to use your hands rather than tongs to hold it. Iron transfers heat slowly, so while the forging end of the bar is glowing hot, the end of the bar you're holding remains relatively cool. A hand grip on your bar is much more secure and allows positive manipulation. Even when you are used to using tongs, it is by far the easiest way to hold and manipulate the stock.

Place the iron into the forge so that the very last 3 or 4 inches are in the fire. You want hot coals both beneath and above the bar so that heat is transferred to the material efficiently. This bed of coal above and below also will help keep the hot steel from oxidizing too much, which will keep scaling to a minimum.

Place the bar on a flat plane in the forge fire, not nose down in the coals. The latter placement will tend to heat the bar unevenly and might burn the end of the bar by being too close to the air blast, which can work like a blowtorch.

Heat the iron slowly and evenly with a steady blast of air. You can watch the progress of your heat by making a small hole with your poker to serve as a view port without overly disturbing the top cover of coals. When the iron is red, it has softened enough to be hammered. Orange heat is much more malleable, however, and is preferable when moving a lot of material; it is easier on your arm as well. Yellow heat is as hot as iron (again, a common name for low-carbon steel) should be taken. After yellow heat comes white hot, and this heat can easily burn steel, injuring it or turning it into a giant sparkler. While this makes a great photo opportunity, it is of no other practical use, as the steel is now beyond repair and must be cut from the bar and discarded.

As you hammer the hot steel, you will find that yellow heat is moved most easily. When orange, it still moves easily under the hammer. As it loses heat and turns to red, the steel starts to become less mal-

## Basic Blacksmithing

leable and more resistant to hammer blows. Soon the steel turns a dull red; this is known as the finishing heat. At this temperature, it is difficult to make any major impact on the shape of the iron, but it serves to even up and smooth out hammer marks from previous, rougher hammering.

Black heat is the next transition during the cooling process, and this heat is indistinguishable from cold iron. It is inadvisable to hit steel at this temperature, as the metal can become brittle and stress fractures can develop. Stress fractures will make the piece especially prone to breaking if it is to be hardened.

Steel has a grain and a memory, and if you were to hammer only one side, the metal's molecules would be compressed on one side only. This might not have a noticeable effect on a piece of iron that is not going to be subjected to the rigors of hardening and tempering, but when you are forging tools, you will find it creates a tendency for the steel to warp. It is a good practice to alternate the sides you forge between heats, keeping a relatively even application of hammer blows from one side to the other. This becomes especially important when forging edged tools.

Black heat looks just like cool steel and is notorious for burning people. It is in excess of 500°F—hot enough to cook your skin if you try to pick it up. Be careful not to leave hot steel sitting about where you will inadvertently grab it. Be careful of others in the shop who might be injured in a similar way. In fact, it's not a bad idea to designate an area specifically for setting steel that is still dangerously hot. This surface should be noncombustible, free of flammable materials, and clearly marked to prevent you or a visitor from being scorched inadvertently. If nothing else, place some bricks on the floor in an out-of-the way corner as a platform for cooling steel.

Have a clear idea what you want to do during each heating and forging session. Once your steel is hot, proceed with dispatch from fire to anvil and shape it with steady, deliberate blows. While the old adage "strike while the iron is hot" is true, it is not a speed competition. Rather, take the time to aim your blows, moving the metal in the direction you want it to go. If it should cool down to the point where it is moving with less ease, put it back in the fire and heat it once again to a good forging heat. Forging the same item might take one smith more heats than another. Go at the pace that suits

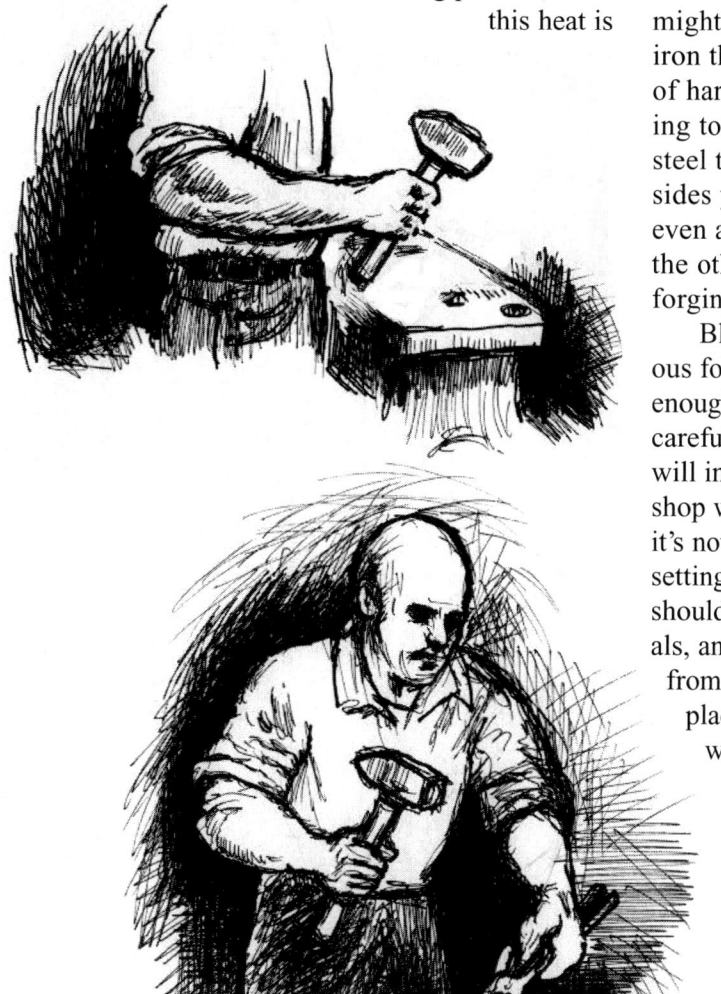

Figure 57. Basic stance working over the anvil.

you—it is better to sacrifice speed than accuracy. Speed will come with time.

Do not lean over the anvil. Missing stock and hitting the hard face of the anvil generates a force that bounces the hammer straight back at you at speeds too fast to dodge or avoid. If your face is in the way, it will be hammered full force, breaking your nose, shattering your teeth, cracking your skull, or rendering you unconscious.

Be sure to take frequent breaks, especially if you are a beginner. Fatigue can be insidious, and you'll be more likely to make a mistake if you work when your muscles are tired.

## HAMMER CONTROL

How to hold the hammer is a matter of personal opinion. Whatever grip is comfortable and allows you control is a good grip. However, you will realize more potential force to your hammer blow the farther down the handle you grasp it.

You will need to hit your hot metal in certain ways to realize the end shape you wish to create. Here are some fundamental techniques to achieve this:

- Using the face of the hammer—Flat blows from the hammer face to the hot iron will move the material in multiple directions, widening and lengthening at the same time it is reducing it in thickness.

- Using the cross peen—Blows from the peen end of the hammer will stretch the metal in the direction you wish to direct it.

- Overhanging blows—Extend the stock over the edge of the anvil and hit with the hammer face half on the metal over the anvil and half on the metal overhanging the edge. This produces a shoulder on the hot metal underneath.

- Glancing blows—Glancing blows direct stock without actually deforming it. A blow from above the iron directs the force downward with very little loss of energy, thus deforming the metal. A glancing blow, by contrast, is delivered from the side and at an angle that delivers less than the full potential force, as the hammer is not stopped by the object struck and its inertia carries it past the point of impact. This causes the metal to move without creating a dent in it.

- Backing-up blows—Backing-up blows are used to upset, or increase the diameter, of the stock—that is, to make it thicker at that point (think of the head of a nail). A backing-up blow is delivered to the very end of the stock as it extends past the edge of the anvil. These blows must be carefully delivered—it's better to use several lighter blows than one heavy blow, since the metal tends to bend if the force isn't delivered precisely along the axis of the stock.

- Shearing blows—Shearing blows land parallel to the anvil's edge, passing close to the edge without touching it. This blow works like a scissors, and the net effect is to cut steel cleanly using just the hammer and anvil edge. The shearing blow is also employed when cutting stock on the hardy chisel. After nicking the stock all around, the last blow of the hammer passes the edge of the hardy, once again like the shearing action of a pair of scissors. Shearing blows require tremendous accuracy, and it is better to avoid the technique until your skills are up to the task. The potential damage to hammers, tools, and anvil edges should be kept in mind. It is a better practice to simply nick the stock all around until it is nearly cut through, then break off the piece while gripping it in a pair of tongs. You will thus avoid the possibility of it shooting off like shrapnel, landing on the floor where it can burn through your boot sole or other such horrible surprise.

## BASIC FORGING TECHNIQUES

Hot iron is remarkably plastic. It can be stretched (drawn), its shape can be changed from round to square to polygonal—almost anything you can imagine. It also can be cut and bent. This amazing malleability gives you an amazing range of forms, but first you have to understand the basic principles behind generating these changes in the metal's form. Read on!

### Drawing Out Iron

When forging a taper to steel, reducing its cross section and increasing its length, you will find that forging a square cross section will allow you to keep the bar straighter and more even. After each hammer blow has delivered its impact to the hot iron, turn the iron 90 degrees and strike again. Rotating the bar that 90 degrees between blows will greatly assist the process of drawing stock evenly and staying square; this helps avoid parallelograms and other unintentional deformations of the hot iron.

If the end taper is to be a round cross section, turn the square taper so that it is on edge (i.e., as a diamond in cross section) and strike a series of blows, once again turning the bar 90 degrees between each. This produces an octagonal cross section, which can then be forged into a round cross section by raining a series of lighter blows along the length of the taper, all the while turning the bar to evenly distribute the blows to the surface of the bar.

### Forming an Acute Point

To forge an acute point on the end of a bar (fig. 58), raise the bar so that the handle end is slightly higher than the level of the anvil and reflecting the opposite angle with your hammer face. You will effectively squeeze the hot steel into the natural declivity thus afforded by the two angles. Turning the bar 90 degrees between blows will quickly form a natural square point. If you extend the tip of the hot steel to the far edge of the anvil, you will avoid the likelihood of your hammer face accidently hitting the anvil face as you draw a sharp point. This is a prelude to forging a scroll end for items like drive-in wall hooks and S hooks.

### Drawing Stock Parallel to the Bar Using the Cross Peen

Using the peen of the hammer effectively in forging takes some getting used to. You are in effect fullering the material (i.e., moving it in a specific direction) in a quick, dynamic way that doesn't require the help of an assistant. It is a quicker but less precise method of fullering the steel than using a hammer and fullering tool, but with a little practice you can approach nearly the same accuracy of moving the metal in the direction you want it to go.

When using the cross peen to fuller steel to the right or left of the bar's length (fig. 59), you want to direct your initial blows to the center of the bar,

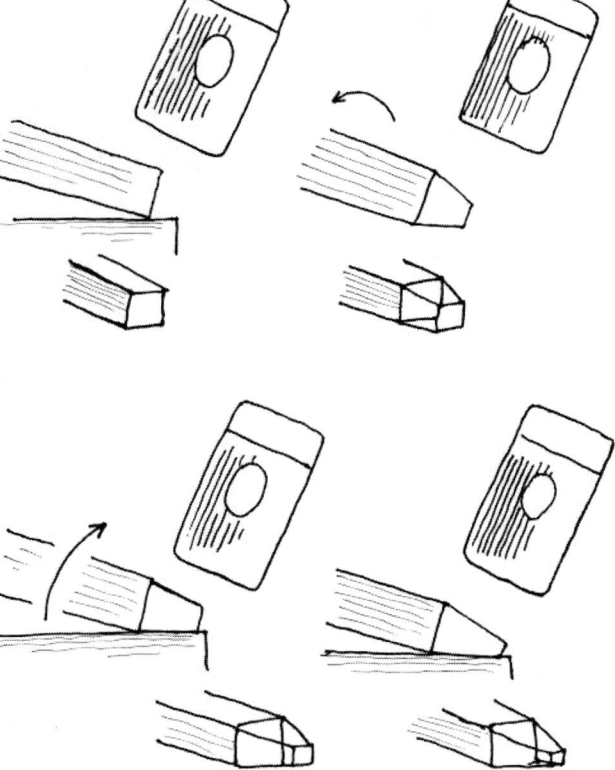

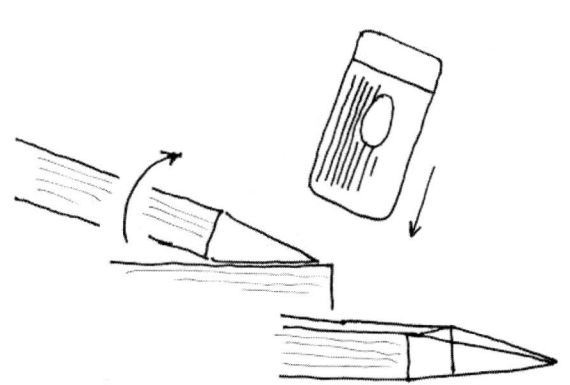

Figure 58. Forging an acute point.

reducing it first. Then, in a series of overlapping blows, direct your steel to the edge of the bar. If you wish to fuller the bar both to the left and right, alternate the blow of the peen, starting in the middle of the stock and working it out both left and right to keep it flowing equally. Drawing in one direction only, as in forging a knife blade that is thick on one edge and thin on the other, will tend to result in a knife bent like a pirate's cutlass: concave on the thick edge and convex on the thin edge. This cannot be corrected after the fact, as that would require hammering on the edge of the knife, thus ruining the sharp edge you just made. Instead, start by bending the bar into a slight curve (imagine a drooping pirate's cutlass), then fullering the convex edge thinner. This will result in the knife straightening out as the edge is thinned.

### Drawing Stock Lengthwise Using the Straight Peen

Again you are using the peen of your hammer to fuller your stock in a single direction, in this case lengthwise. Starting where the iron needs to be thickest, work outward with increasing force of blows, slightly overlapping each divot formed and reducing your stock by degrees as it increases in length. Wider peens tend to draw the stock with less chance of forming folds in the iron being drawn out.

The cross peen can accomplish this task, but because it is at a right angle to the hammer handle, you will find your hand is directly over the hot iron. The straight peen is the better choice. Because its fuller is in line with the handle, you are working with your hand at right angles to and away from the hot metal being drawn out.

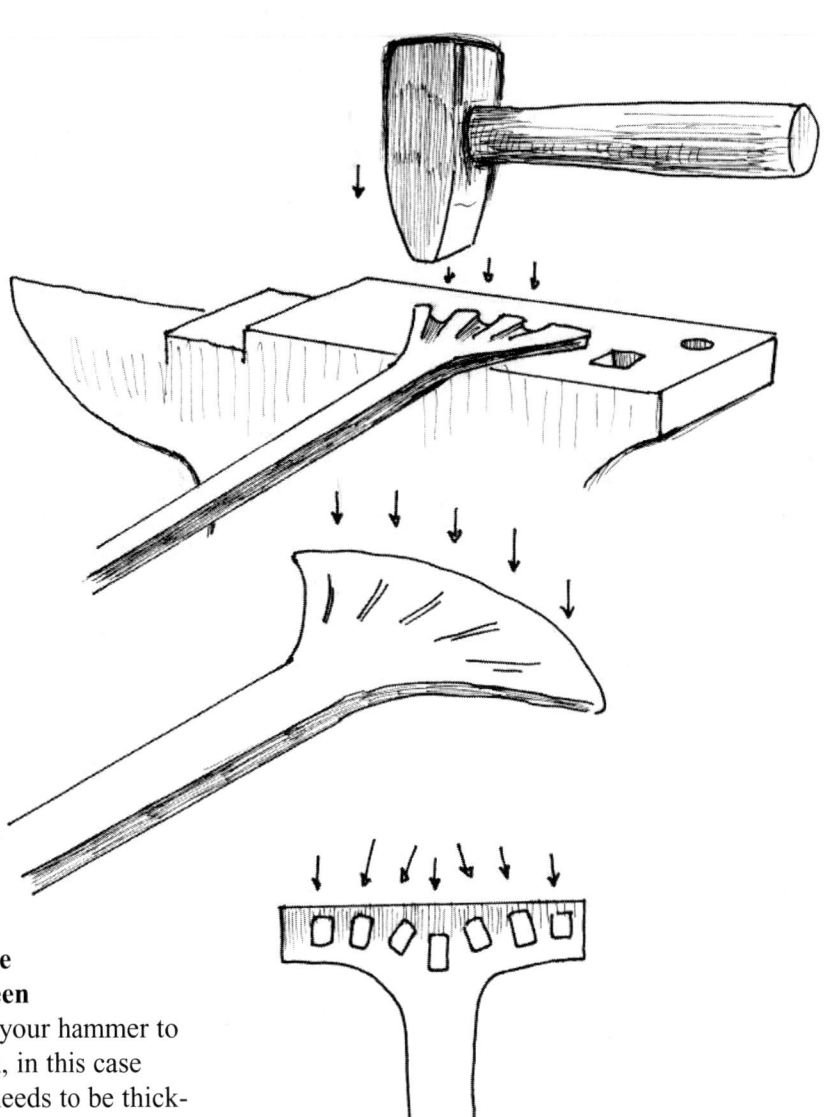

Figure 59. Drawing stock parallel to the bar.

### Cutting on the Hardy Chisel

When cutting stock on the hardy chisel (fig. 60), you are not trying to cut clean through in one blow. Rather, you want to nick the bar all about with a series of blows, but none so forceful as to cut through the stock completely. Ideally, you want to cut the stock just deep enough to weaken it so that a final light blow will cause the stock to break off the end of the bar. If you were to attempt to cut through the bar

## Basic Blacksmithing

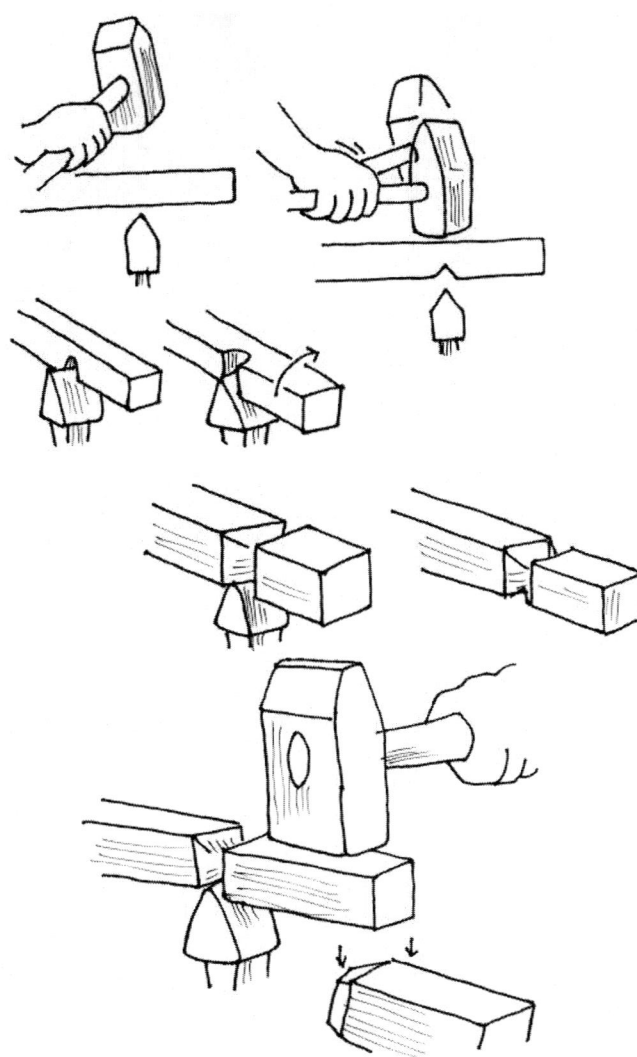

Figure 60. Cutting on the hardy chisel.

all in one go, you would damage either your hammer face, the hardy chisel edge, or both.

### Bending Hot Steel

Acute bends can be accomplished by locking the hot iron in a vise, then pulling the protruding stock downward with tongs while assisting the bend with hammer blows to the stock over the anvil jaw. Radial bends like ring and S-hook bends are more gradual and can be formed on the horn of the anvil or over a cone mandrel, or by extending the hot iron over the edge of the anvil and striking glancing blows with the hammer face. Tapered stock, especially long, gradual tapers, has a natural tendency to form radial bends and scroll shapes.

### Forming a Shoulder

Overhanging blows are used to form a shoulder on the underside of the stock. Place the hot iron so it extends past the edge of the anvil and aim a blow so that the hammer face strikes half on the stock on the anvil and half on the stock extending past the edge. This technique uses the edge of the anvil like an upside-down set hammer to forge a crisp shoulder on the iron.

### Forming a Ring Bend

When bending rings (fig. 61), support one end of the stock on the anvil horn and forge the hot iron downward without actually hammering it against the horn. This will guide the iron downward into a curved shape. Reverse the stock so the tongs grip

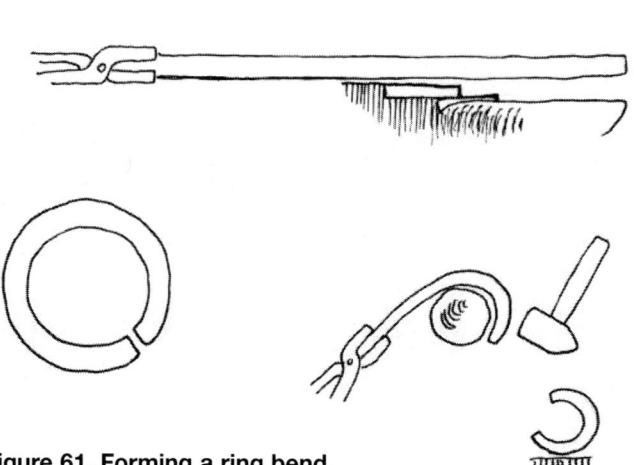

Figure 61. Forming a ring bend.

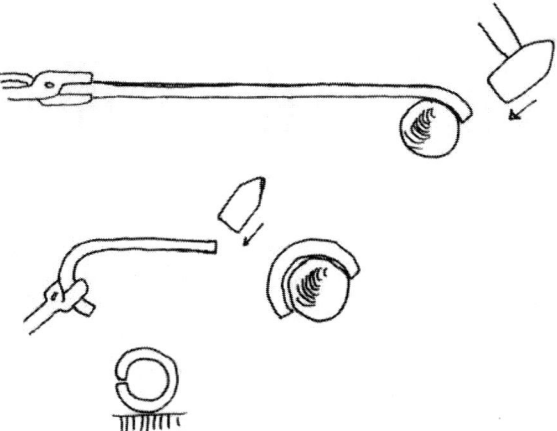

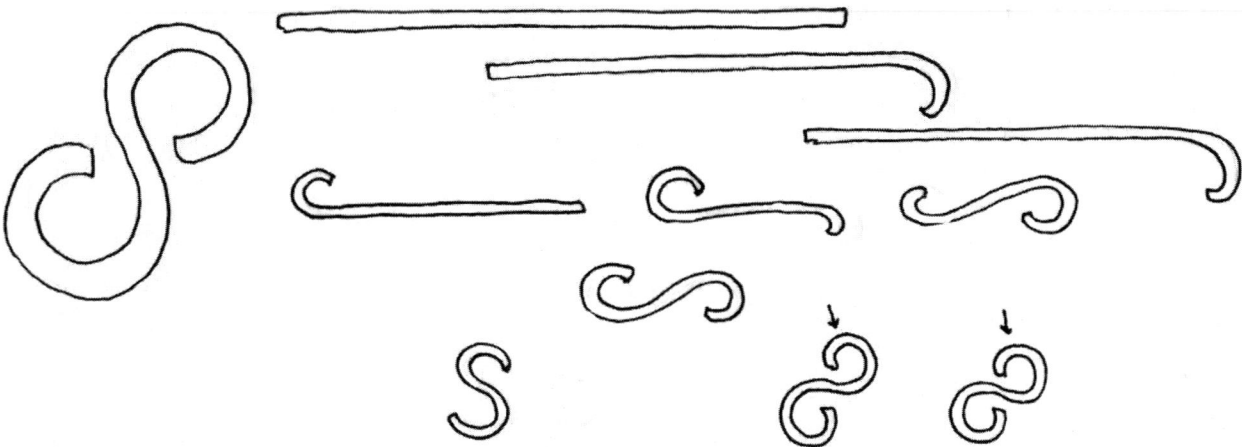

Figure 62. Forming an S bend.

the portion just formed and repeat the process in the same way and direction. Close the ring on the face of the anvil and true up its shape on the horn.

### Forming an S Bend

The S bend is produced like the ring bend (fig. 62). However, when you get to the stage of forging the opposite end of the bar, turn the bar 180 degrees and proceed.

### Forming an Eye Bend

To form an eye bend (fig. 63), lay out enough stock to produce the eye and forge the steel with glancing blows over the far edge of the anvil so that it is bent 90 degrees relative to the bar. Extend the very end of this bent section over the anvil horn and forge it into a downward curve. Place the piece back onto the anvil face and strike with angled blows to direct the eye into a closed circle.

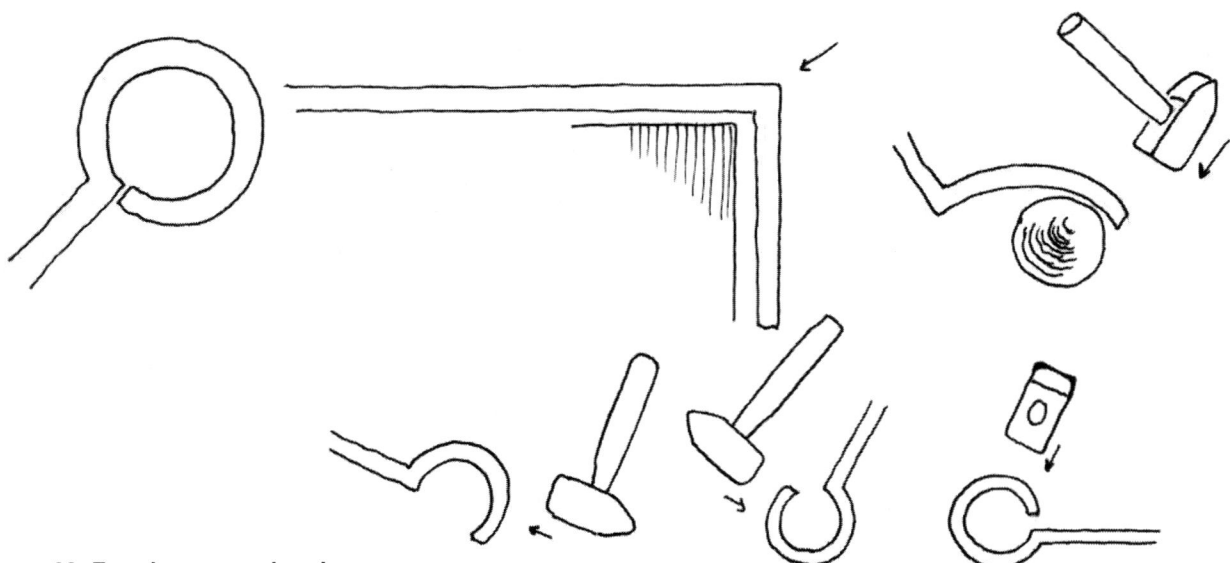

Figure 63. Forming an eye bend.

## Basic Blacksmithing

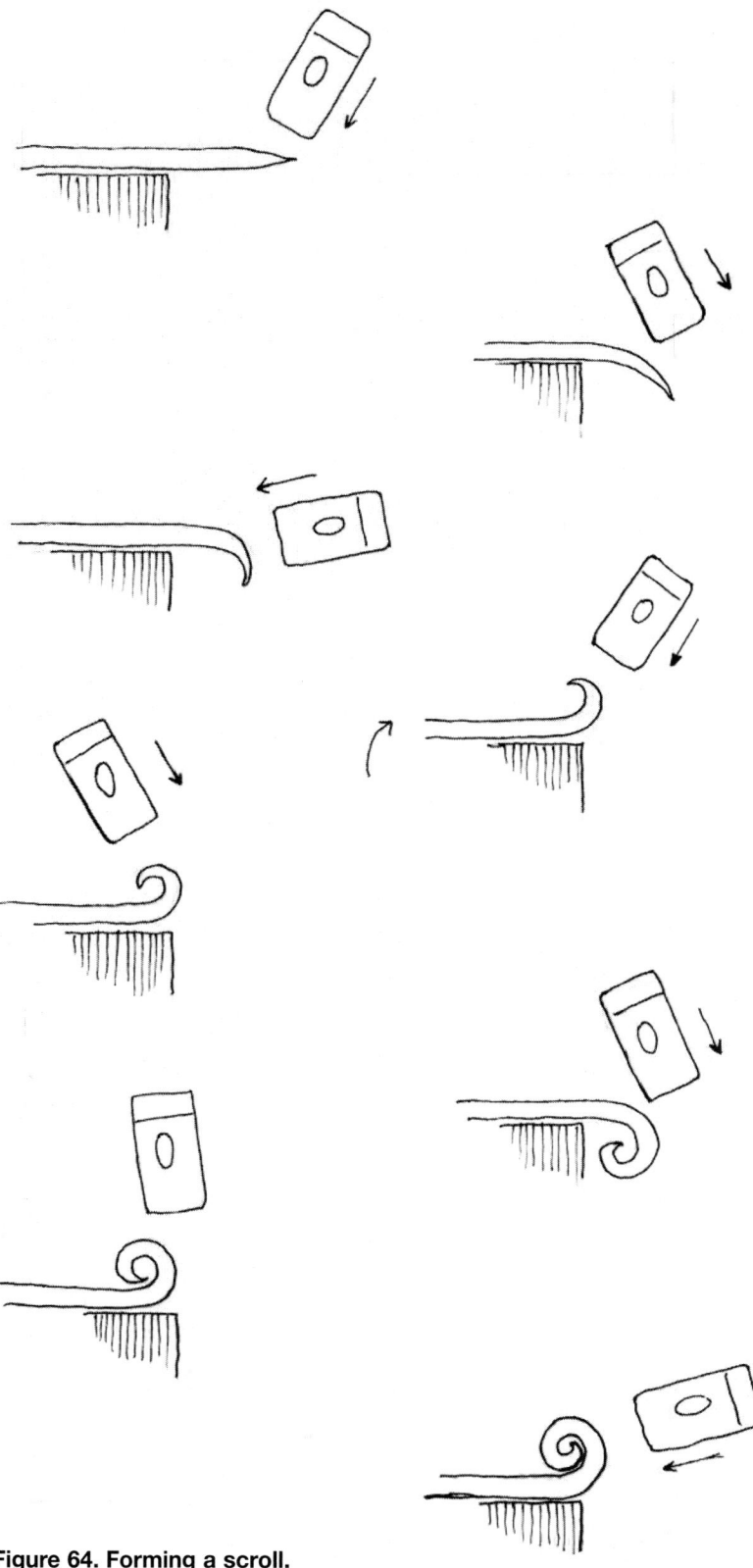

Figure 64. Forming a scroll.

### Forming a Scroll

Whether you are scrolling flat, square, or round stock, the key to forging scrolls (fig. 64) is the taper. Scrolls form naturally when stock has a gentle, even taper. Divots and uneven transitions in cross section will kink and bend and will not produce a satisfactory natural scroll.

Start by forging a square taper on the end of a bar. Rotate the bar 45 degrees and forge the corners down to an octagonal cross section; then continue to turn and forge the rod until you have a round cross section.

Extend your tapered stock till the thinnest part overhangs the edge of the anvil. With a few tapping blows to the tip, and with the anvil edge forming a fulcrum, the stock begins to scroll into a J shape. Turn the stock 180 degrees, rest it on the far side of the anvil face, and gently hammer the J downward and into itself, forming a P shape and then a tighter scroll. Repeat these two steps, laying your scroll end over the anvil and forging the scroll tighter and larger until the scroll is the size you like.

## The Book of Blacksmithing

**Forming a Sharp Corner Bend**

There is a trick to producing visually square corner bends without upsetting the stock (fig. 65). While this technique is not suitable for all forgings, it has its application in some work. Where strength is an issue, such as the bend on andiron legs or gate work, upsetting the stock at the area to be forged to a sharp corner bend will likely be the best means of proceeding.

Lay the amount of stock you wish bent over the edge of the anvil and strike glancing blows to the end of the bar, directing it down and inward toward the anvil's side. Now strike the iron alternately toward the side of the anvil and on top toward its face, starting a right angle bend. There is no need to hit it hard—you don't want to deform the iron, just direct it.

Next, lay the bent iron on its side so it looks like the number 7. Strike the top corner at a 45-degree angle, pulling the stock outward. This makes the bend look sharper. Now lay the stock over the edge of the anvil so it is snug to the far edge and hammer both the top and side of the corner. This will produce a bend that looks sharp and square.

**Forming an Edge**

Edge forming is used extensively in forging tools, from chisels to knife edges. For chisels, it is best to forge their blades by extending the steel to the far edge of the anvil and lifting the stock slightly so the handle end is higher than the hot end you are about to hammer. If you reflect the angle produced by the position of the steel on the anvil, you will, with an economy of effort, produce a chisel edge. This technique is similar to forging an acute point, but you are only forging two sides to the chisel blade rather than turning the bar repeatedly and forging from all directions.

**Forging a Penny Foot**

A penny foot is a flat, bent section on the end of a bar that's used, for example, as an attachment plate on wall hooks. It can also form the feet on items like candleholders and trivets.

To make a penny foot (fig. 66), shoulder the

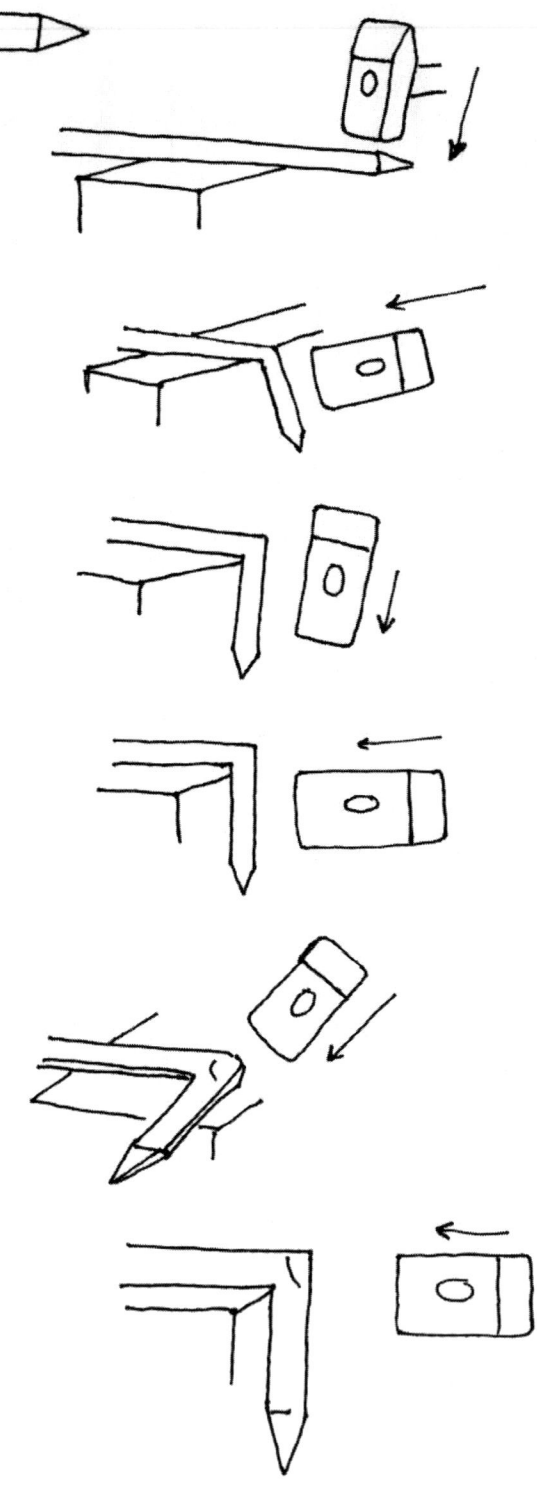

Figure 65. Forming a sharp corner without upsetting the stock.

stock at the end of a bar with an overhanging blow, laying off about the same length as the diameter of the bar to give you a square of material adjacent to your shoulder. Widen and thin this section into a trapezoid; then hold it on edge on the anvil face and forge with light blows to form a hexagon from the trapezoid, and then a circle from the hexagon. Turn the bar so it is once again resting flat on the anvil face, with the shoulder edge snugged to the near edge of the anvil, and hammer smooth and flat. Rotate the bar so the shouldered edge is uppermost and position so the penny foot hangs over edge of anvil. Using light blows, bend the penny foot downward to form a right angle from the bar. If you are making an attachment plate for a wall hook, punch or drill a hole for a mounting nail or screw.

### Truing Up Forgings

Once steel is drawn out using the peen of the hammer, it must be further forged to even up and blend the deformations caused by the rounded surface of the peen (unless the ridged surface thus produced is desired). Use straight downward blows with the hammer face to forge the stock to an even surface.

### Punching Hot Steel

When you punch hot steel, whether it is thick or thin, it is best to punch halfway through. By turning the stock 180 degrees, you will briefly be able to see a darker spot on the surface of the hot iron. This is caused by the brief cooling of the stock where the punch has compressed the steel. This dark spot will quickly fade as the heat surrounding it is absorbed. You can use this mark as a means of locating the spot to position your punch to once again drive into the hot iron without going all the way through. After counterpunching the iron, again turn the stock 180 degrees and punch out the resulting plug of compressed steel over the pritchel hole of the anvil. If the pritchel hole is

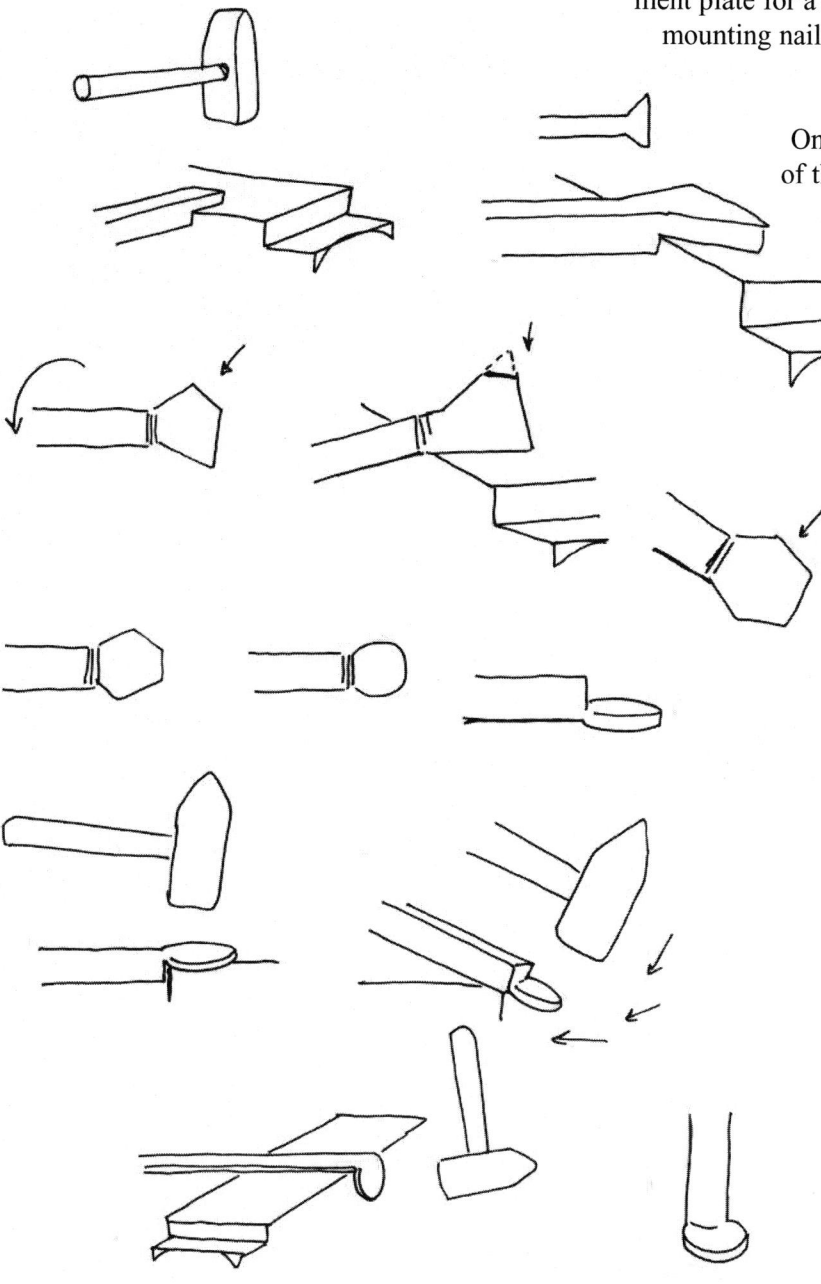

Figure 66. Forging a penny foot.

too small, use the hardy hole. You will find that if this last step is performed with the stock cooled to a black heat, the plug cuts a bit more easily.

**Truing Up a Punched Hole Using a Drift Pin**

Use a drift pin to true up the sides of stock that have bulged out when creating a hole. This happens frequently when punching bars of large stock, such as when forming the eyes of handled tools.

Once the hole has been punched to the desired size, drive in a drift pin to match the shape of the intended handle. The best way to do this is to tap the drift pin into the hole until it doesn't wobble, then quickly drive it through the hole with greater force. If you allow the drift to remain in the hole long enough to heat up, it will expand and stick in there. Keep the drift moving throughout the following procedures. Lay the hot steel on its side with the drift pin in place and true up the sides with hammer blows. Drive the drift out in between heats and cool it in water so it does not overheat, which can deform it and cause it to stick in the hole. The drift heats up quickly, so as you drive it out of the eye of the tool you are forming, do not attempt to pick it up in your bare hands. Use tongs to pick it up to quench and reinsert into the eye of the tool you are forming.

**Splitting Hot Steel with a Slit Chisel and Vise**

When splitting steel, begin by cutting straight down into the stock using a robust chisel against a cutting plate. Cut on one side of the hot stock, then turn the bar over and cut into the other side (fig. 67). This forms a chisel cut, beveled on both sides, and keeps the stock more even in cross section. If you were to cut with the chisel from one side only, your split would yield stock that is thinner at the top of the

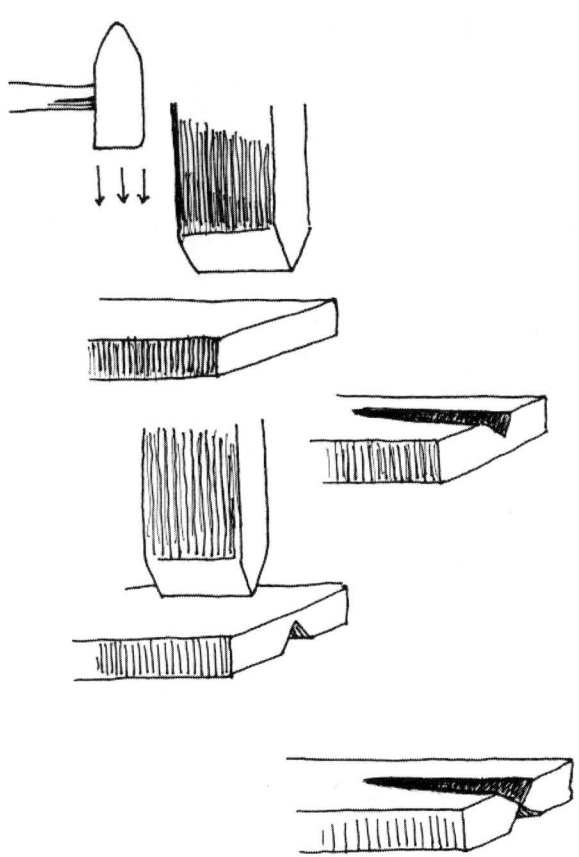

Figure 67. Splitting hot steel.

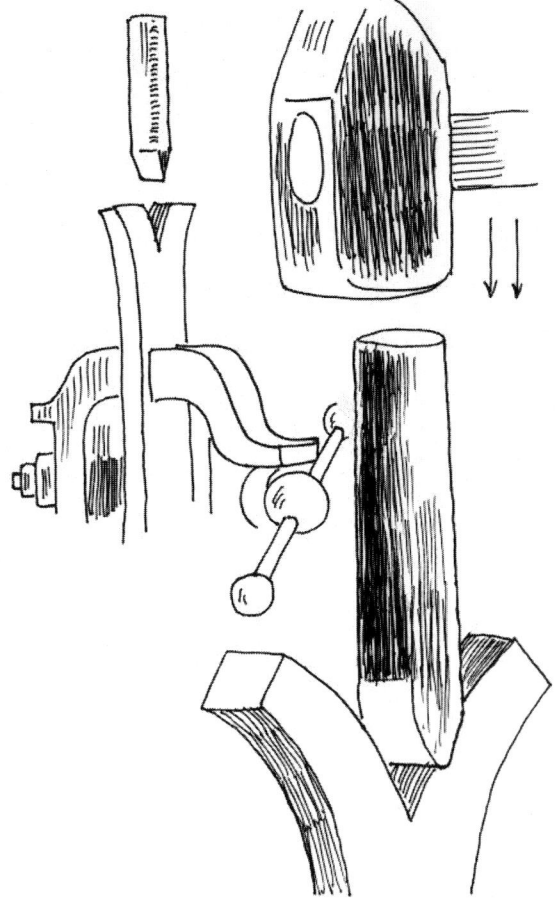

Figure 68. Splitting hot steel (cont.).

cut and wider at the bottom. Locking the hot steel in a vise, you then drive a thin-edged chisel, called a slitting chisel, down into the split previously cut by the robust chisel (fig. 68). Cutting with the slit chisel down into the split opens it up slightly as the stock is forced apart and leaves a clean, tapered cut. If the split section is to be developed further, as when forging the tines of a flesh fork, follow the splitting chisel operation with a thin fuller chisel, developing a clean, gentle curve to the inside of the split stock.

### Fullering Split Stock

As described above, split stock can be opened up and the inside of the cut shaped and developed using hand chisel fullers. Start with thin fullers and gradually work the stock wider with increasingly wider fullers.

### Finish Hammering

Once the steel has been hammered to shape and all major forging steps are completed, you can smooth out any marks from the hammer face by heating the steel to a dull red and hammering the metal to a smooth, even surface. A dull red heat does not allow for a great deal of deformation; thus the hammer blows applied at this heat do not move the metal very much.

## HEAT TREATING

The harder they are, the more brittle they become. This is particularly true of the high-carbon steels. Heat treating, or tempering, allows you to adjust your work's final hardness though a controlled reheating and cooling of the metal.

When forging low-carbon steel, heat treating is not an issue. Iron will harden somewhat if it is hammered cold, as will nonferrous metals; this is called work hardening. Work hardening is accomplished by carefully hammering cold metal so that the surface becomes packed tighter. It will toughen low-carbon steel, but there is a limit to how much work hardening can be accomplished, as eventually the work will become overly brittle and stress fracture.

### Hardening Steel

Steel with a carbon content over 50 points (or ½ a percent carbon content) has sufficient carbon in it to harden. Medium-carbon steels range from around 50 points carbon up to 70 points. High-carbon steel can range anywhere from 80 to 120 points. The higher the carbon content in steel, the harder it will become. Steel with less than 30 points of carbon will usually not harden appreciably.

Steel with sufficient carbon content can be heated until it is no longer responsive to magnetic attraction, at which point cooling quickly by quenching will render it hard and brittle. The heat at which medium- and high-carbon steels become nonmagnetic varies with the amount of carbon the steel contains. The higher the carbon content, the lower the temperature at which it will successfully harden. Higher carbon content will also affect the degree of hardness obtainable through tempering. Different steels have characteristic heat signatures: brighter orange and less bright for lower carbon steels, decreasing in temperature to red heats for steels of higher carbon content.

Carbon steels have a grain that requires they be worked in a fairly narrow heat range. The higher the carbon, the more narrow that range becomes. Medium-carbon steels have the widest working range, from a low red up to an orange heat. Very high-carbon steels are best worked in a red to a bright red heat.

Overheating carbon steel is damaging to the grain structure of the metal. The grains become more enlarged and coarse as heat is increased, and the longer this heat is allowed to soak into the steel, the more this grain growth will continue. Hammering steel helps to break these crystals down to smaller size. Thus when working high-carbon steel, initial shaping is done at a higher heat and finish hammering at a much lower heat. Hitting cold steel is as injurious to the grain as overheating and will promote stress fractures in the steel, which will lead to the steel cracking as it is hardened. To avoid this, do not hammer carbon steel at below red heat. When hardening steel, do not heat it for longer than it needs to completely reach its critical hardening temperature.

Once steel is hardened, it is as brittle as glass, and some of this brittleness needs to be removed by tempering, which is a controlled reheating of the steel to between 400°F and 600°F. Once steel is hardened, be aware that until it is tempered, hitting, dropping, or bending it will in all likelihood lead to breaking it, so handle it gently.

### Quench Mediums

The two basic quenches I work with are water and vegetable oil. Each quench medium is contained in a steel vessel big enough to quickly cool the largest item I am likely to need to harden, with enough head space in the container to allow for the mass of the object to be fully immersed without overflowing the container.

My water quench tank is an old 30-gallon steel drum, as is my oil quench tank. My oil quench has a lid of sheet iron so that any flash fire can be deprived of air if the oil should overheat or flash out of control. When quenching hot steel in oil, you will need to immerse the steel past the area that is red hot. If you linger at the surface of the oil with red hot steel, the surface will ignite—that is, it will flash fire. This will normally go out immediately as you plunge the hot steel below the surface, but you obviously do not want to be standing directly over the quench container, nor do you want your arms or hands over it. Because of the potential of being burned by the flash, use long-handled tongs with a good grip on your steel. Tongs with a positive grip will also help you get hold of an item in the quench tank; it can be a challenge trying to grip a slippery piece in the bottom of an oily mess.

When quenching your steel in oil, you can avoid warping it by plunging the item straight into the bath and keeping it immersed. Plunge it up and down so it keeps in contact with cool oil. The same applies when quenching in water, but this time you're preventing a blanket of steam from surrounding the steel and interfering with the speed of cooling.

Use water to quench water-hardening (W series) steels and oil to quench oil-hardening (O series) steels. If you are in any doubt as to what kind of steel you have, test a small piece before you spend the time and effort forging a tool, only to crack it by quenching it in the wrong medium.

### TEMPERING

Tempering steel is accomplished by carefully reheating hardened steel to a low heat range to remove some of its brittleness and to impart more flexibility to the metal. This renders it less susceptible to fracture and breaking from shock and torque force. Medium-carbon steel can be tempered to be very tough and flexible and is therefore the steel of choice for springs and tools that must have toughness as well as the ability to flex and return to their original form. Tempering medium-carbon steel to about 500°F renders the material very resistant to shock but removes a lot of the hardness and edge-holding characteristics.

To attain a hard-edged tool with the maximum of shock resistance and flexibility, differential tempering is employed. The steel is tempered—that is, heated until the right temper color appears—according to the temperatures in the following chart. Straw yellow results in the hardest but still brittle steel and is used for cutting edges that must be hard. Gold is tougher (i.e., less brittle) but still very hard. Reddish brown is tough and hard; full or peacock blue tougher still but less hard; and finally dark or deep blue, which is more tough yet but holds an edge for less time in use. Blue tempers are less hard but much more resistant to breaking.

| Temper Colors and Temperatures | |
|---|---|
| Light yellow—straw | 440°F |
| Straw | 460°F |
| Gold—deep straw | 470°F |
| Yellow brown | 490°F |
| Bronze | 500°F |
| Reddish brown | 520°F |
| Purple | 540°F |
| Dark purple | 550°F |
| Full blue | 560°F |
| Dark blue | 570°F |

The technique is as follows. Once the tool has been hardened and is cool enough to touch, degrease it with a rag to make cleaning easier. Brighten the surface with emery paper; then, using a self-sparking propane torch, heat the tool from the end that the hammer strikes (the handle end) until the temper colors appear. Direct and guide the heat of the torch as you gradually heat from the handle end toward the tool tip (the working end). As the heat travels from the handle end to the tip, the colors will travel in specific bands. The leading color will be gold, followed by reddish brown, light blue, peacock blue, and dark blue. Be careful to not go past the blue range, as you don't want to accidentally reharden the handle end of the tool, which needs to be the softest and toughest portion. When the temper color you want has reached the tip, quench the tool immediately in water to prevent softening the metal beyond that point. Water is used as a quenching medium after tempering for all steels, as tempering heats are much cooler than forging heats.

In the projects in chapter 7, I refer to this tempering process by saying "temper to light blue" or "temper to bronze." This instruction means to quench the tool when that color band, traveling from the handle end, has reached the tool tip.

Tools intended for forging cold iron, such as a center punch or a cold-cutting hardy, should be tempered to reddish brown. Tools such as chisels and punches should be tempered to a blue color. Knives and wood-carving tools are best if the back of the blade is tempered blue and the cutting edge only heated enough to allow a gold or straw color to appear. This is the hardness at which a new file will cut, not skate off, the surface, resulting in a blade that can be sharpened by a file or grinding tool.

## ANNEALING

Carbon steel that has been heated and allowed to cool down at room temperature is referred to as normalized. Although it isn't hardened, it will be difficult to machine in this condition, being harder to file and likely to break drill bits and saw blade teeth. In order to work carbon steel effectively—to be able to file it, drill it, or cut it with hacksaws, etc.—it needs to be annealed. This process is like hardening, in that the steel must be heated to its critical temperature, but instead of quenching it to cool it suddenly, you want to do just the opposite: cool it gradually. High-carbon steel can be rendered as soft as iron if, after being heated to the nonmagnetic point, it is allowed to cool very slowly. The slower the heat dissipates from the steel, the softer it will become. Thus you need some way to insulate the steel from cooling too fast.

One way to accomplish this is to bury the steel in an iron box filled with dry wood ashes, which will serve to insulate the hot steel and allow it to cool slowly. Vermiculite, the same stuff used in gardening, will also insulate the steel very well and allow it to cool slowly enough to reach dead soft.

If you are annealing a small piece that is likely to lose its heat too quickly, or if you are working in very cold weather, a good trick to ensure enough time for gradual cooling of the steel is to first bury a large piece of iron heated orange hot in your annealing container. Layer some of your insulation under and over it, then heat and bury your workpiece on top of the wood ash or vermiculite, with plenty of the insulation on top to conserve the heat. Leaving it overnight will help you resist the temptation to remove the steel too soon.

Annealing small stock for up to 8 hours is usually sufficient; larger stock can be annealed for up to 12 or more hours. When the steel is cool to the touch, test it with a file. If the file cuts the stock as easily as it cuts mild steel, you have successfully annealed your high-carbon steel. After you have finished all the shaping and finishing, drilling, and filing, the steel can be hardened and then tempered according to the carbon content and the eventual use the tool is intended to serve.

## TWISTING HOT STEEL

Hot iron is a joy to work with—a normally intractable, obdurate material that suddenly, as if by magic, becomes plastic and tractable. It is both exciting and intoxicating. When iron is hot, it is like a stiff clay, and all sorts of wonderful shaping options open up to the smith.

One of the simplest means of decorating iron is by twisting it (fig. 69). The simplest twists are accomplished by taking iron of square cross section and, once heated to a good orange heat, securing one end in a vise; grasping the protruding portion with an adjustable wrench, vise grips, or tongs; and simply turning the material clockwise or counterclockwise. With very little effort, you will see the ordinary square iron transform into an attractive twist. If you continue to twist, you will tighten the piece more and more until it resembles the threading of a machined screw. If you were to continue much further, however, you would find that, even if you were still at a bright red heat, the twist would eventually break off the bar. This is the point known as twist shear. Usually there is a count of how many twists you can safely fit into a certain length and diameter of stock. While I have never been so thorough as to compute this relationship mathematically, I have over the years gained an instinctive sense of when enough is enough, usually by twisting off a piece or two by too zealous effort on my part. The ease of twisting hot iron can be controlled by the heat you apply to your stock—the more heat applied, the easier it is to twist the stock. Twists can also be controlled by judiciously cooling areas you have already manipulated with the assistance of a small watering can.

Here is a rundown of some different twists and how they are accomplished.

- Plain square stock twist—As previously discussed, a sim-

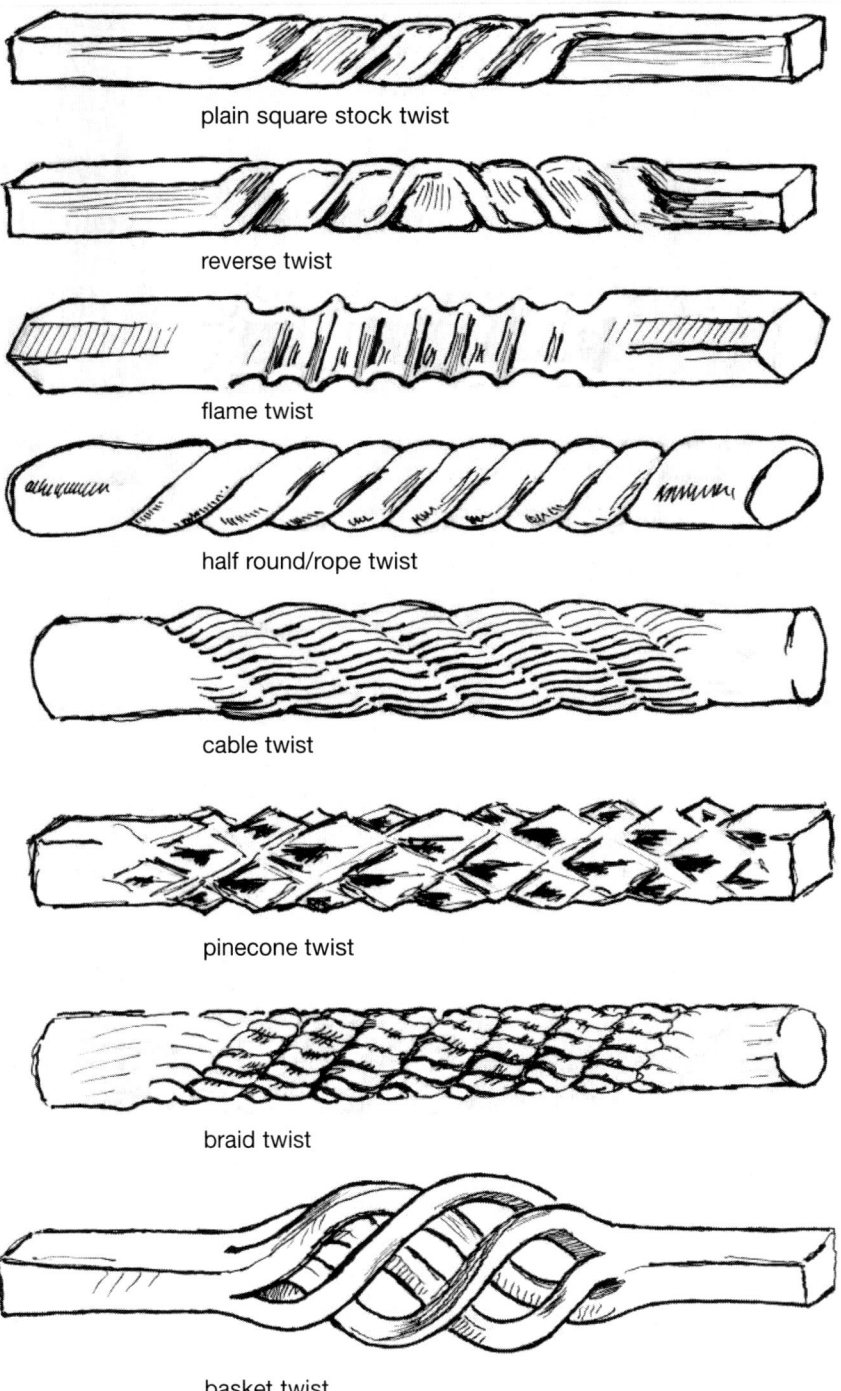

Figure 69. Twists.

ple twist is executed by locking square cross-sectioned iron in a vise and turning with a tool, rotating the hot stock until you achieve the degree of twist you find most appealing. An even heat helps ensure an even twist.

- Reverse twist—This twist, while in effect as simple as the above twist, looks awesome. By twisting hot iron first clockwise and then, farther down the bar, reversing the twist counterclockwise, you get a twist that undulates across the surface.

- Flame twist—The same as the simple twist but with an extra forging step. Forge a square bar flat on two sides by setting the bar on the anvil face so it is in diamond cross section and flattening the top and bottom edges of the diamond at the same time. Secure the hot iron in the vise and twist. This technique gives a multilayer effect to the twist.

- Half round or rope twist—If you twist round stock, you see no appreciable surface change. However, round stock can produce some lovely twist patterns by the simple expedient of first flattening one side of the stock so it is flat on two sides and half round on the two opposing sides. When this stock is twisted, it gives the surface impression of twisted rope.

- Cable twist—Multiple small bars of round stock, when twisted together hot, give a wire rope or cable effect.

- Pinecone twist—This twist is a little more labor intensive, but it gives a remarkable surface treatment, ending up with a series of raised diamonds over the entire twisted section. Start by doing the simple twist with stock of square cross section. Once twisted, reheat the bar and forge it into a square cross section. Then, gripping it in the vise, turn it counter to the original twist. As it untwists, little diamond shapes start to pop to the surface.

- Braid twist—This is one of the more elaborate twists. Start by taking seven pieces of small-diameter round stock of perhaps 3 feet in length, fold each in half, and twist tightly—the tighter the better, but avoiding overtwisting and shearing. Repeat this step until you have seven pieces all twisted in the same direction. Gather the pieces together and lock one end of the bundle securely in a vise. Grasp the other end of the bundle with a pair of vise grips and then twist in the opposite direction of the original twist. This produces a lovely woven pattern on the resulting rod's surface.

- Basket twist—Weld together an odd number of small round stock, of about 12 inches in length, on both ends, using perhaps an inch of weld on either end. Lock in the vise and twist while exerting slight pressure down toward the vise. As the rods twist, they will also open up, producing an open basketwork effect.

## FORGE WELDING BASICS

Back in the heyday of smithing, before the twentieth century, welding was accomplished in the forge fire by heating the iron until it was nearly white and then fusing it between the hammer and anvil. If the iron was properly scarfed (see below) and the heat was sufficient, the welded joint was as strong as the material it was made from. This was in part due to the low carbon and the presence of silica in the wrought iron that formed at high heat a flux of glass that served to keep oxygen at bay and helped to inhibit the formation of scale. In the twentieth century, the introduction of mild steel as the prevalent material for forging created a problem for the old smiths used to working with wrought iron. They claimed that no good weld could be obtained from this new material, due, in part, to the higher carbon content and lack of silica in mild steel.

### Preparation and Basic Hammering

Smiths began to treat mild steel as they had high-carbon steel and added a flux to the hot metal before welding it. This flux—which might consist of sand, borax, or combinations of borax and iron filings—serves the same purpose that the silica had, preventing atmospheric oxygen from combining with the hot steel, thus keeping it free of scale so that molten steel would contact the same.

Picture, if you will, a piece of wax paper between two layers of clay. No matter how you try to squish the clay together, the thin paper forms a shim, a mechanical barrier, that prevents the clay's surfaces from adhering and combining with each other. Remove the wax paper, however, and the clay becomes one with easy pressure. Flux prevents a similar barrier of scale from forming, thus allowing the two pieces of steel to fuse.

To achieve the best results when forge welding mild steel, you need to properly scarf the ends of the bars to be welded and flux the surfaces to be heated to welding heat. Clean surfaces with a wire brush before adding flux. Borax seems to work best for all general flux applications. You then transfer the semi-molten surfaces to the anvil with dispatch to not lose the welding heat and apply the first few blows with restraint to tack the pieces together. You then forge with more robust blows as you proceed to shoot out any adhering scale and thoroughly fuse the pieces. At times you will need additional welding heat and subsequent hammering to achieve a completed weld. The initial blows are gentle so you do not force the hot pieces apart, shooting one piece out of contact with the other.

### Scarfing

To weld two pieces, it is best to slightly taper each end to be welded to form a more easily blended join, a process known as scarfing (fig. 70). Forge welding without tapered ends leaves a gap or hairline and makes the weld structurally weak and prone to fail when subjected to bending force. The object of scarfing is to shape the ends to be welded so they are slightly convex; this allows the two pieces to fuse in the center first and any scale to be shot out the sides. Any hollow area, gap, or declivity that could trap scale would likely interfere with the molten metal's ability to fuse together and produce a weak weld, or a weld that fuses only partially.

To scarf flat stock, prepare the ends to be welded by heating the very tips to a good forging heat. Set the end of the bar on the far edge of the anvil and, with a series of backing-up blows, upset the iron till it is somewhat thicker than its original mass. Now forge the end of the bar to a blunt, abrupt chisel edge with a slightly convex surface. Again, this convex surface is important, as the object of scarfing the steel is to allow the hot metal to meet so that the center portions fuse first. This allows any foreign material to be driven out of the sides as the weld takes.

Fusing round stock by forge welding involves a slightly different scarfing method. As with flat stock, heat just the very end of the bar and extend the bar to the far end of the anvil face. Use backing-up blows to upset the stock, increasing its thickness. Now, instead of a blunt chisel end, forge an acute point. Round the top slightly to once again ensure that the hot steel

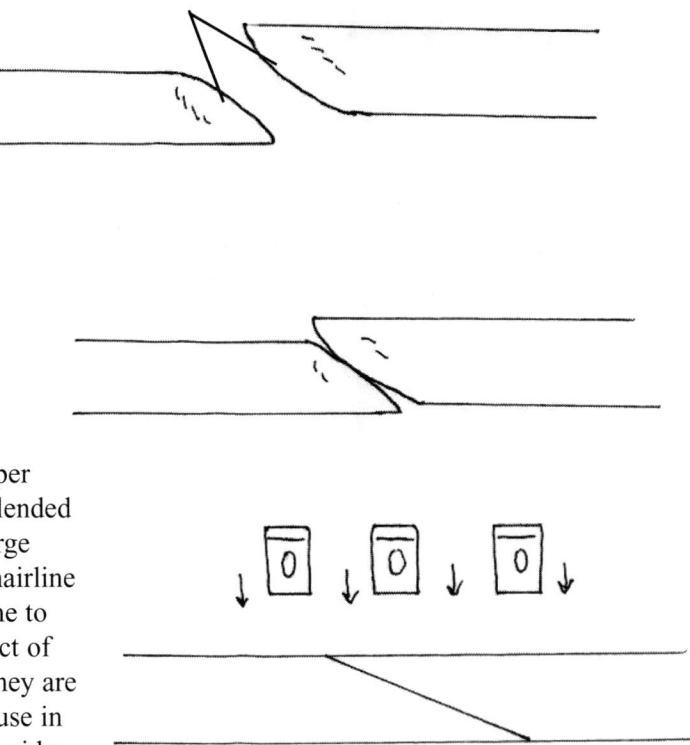

Figure 70. Scarfing.

will meet at the center of the stock to be welded. The pointed end of this scarf blends itself more readily when welding round stock, where a chisel point would take more effort to blend into the weld, requiring more hammer blows and potentially leaving a crease in the welded area, which might weaken it.

There is a trick to positioning two pieces of scarfed iron for welding. One bar is placed on the anvil scarf upward. The unmodified end of the other bar is rested near the edge of the anvil face scarf downward and, from that fulcrum point, lowered into position on top of the bottom piece. A few taps to tack the weld are followed by increasing force of hammer blows.

### Forge Welding Low-Carbon Steel

Forge welding low-carbon steel is best done at a heat just below bright yellow. If you see a couple of sparks from the fire, it is time to strike, because the iron is hot!

Low-carbon steel will weld at a bright orange heat, but it is slippery and prone to slide apart at the first hammer blows. Taking the iron up to a good yellow heat and a little beyond will make it grab immediately.

Two pieces of iron need to be the same temperature for welding. A simple technique to achieve this is to lay the stock to be joined next to (but not touching) each other in the fire. This will bring both parts up to welding temperature simultaneously. Be careful how you place your piece when ready to weld, as once it touches the other surface, it will stick and you are committed to welding where it has adhered.

### Forge Welding Medium-Carbon Steel

Spring steel welds at a lower heat than iron. Taking medium-carbon steel up to the same temperature as iron to weld will result in the spring steel burning and crumbling as it is struck with the hammer, shooting sparks and particles of hot burned steel all about the shop. Spring steel welds to itself at a little bit above a bright orange heat—its surface looks as if swirling butter is melting on it.

Medium-carbon steel welds easily to mild steel. Preheating the iron to its welding heat while the spring steel arrives at its lower heat is the best method, but iron will also weld to the medium-carbon steel at the spring steel's welding heat.

Some tools, such as a cold-cutting chisel, need both a hard cutting or working end and a shock-resistant handle or body. The elements of hardness and resilience can be combined in one piece by welding medium-carbon steel to a mild steel, or you can selectively temper medium-carbon steel so that the same piece is hardened at the working end (tempered) and softened (annealed) on the other. Both techniques have their merits, and it's difficult to say which is simpler. It may come down to individual preference: some people are more comfortable with the welding technique, while others find selective tempering and annealing to be the easier and more satisfying approach.

### Forge Welding High-Carbon Steel

High-carbon steel needs even less heat to weld than spring steel, low to bright orange heat usually being sufficient when dealing with 100-point steel. When combining dissimilar carbon contents, try to stay closer to the lowest welding heat of the highest carbon material being welded. This will avoid overheating and burning the higher carbon component of the two elements being combined.

# CHAPTER 6

# Troubleshooting
## What Went Wrong and How to Fix It

Blacksmithing requires strength, spatial judgment, and a high degree of physical coordination. Until you've acquired these skills, you'll make mistakes estimating things like time, temperature, and the force needed to do the job. But mixed in with these frustrations will be the joy of learning a fascinating craft! This chapter explores some of the problems you'll encounter on the way and how to deal with them.

### PARALLELOGRAMS

Steel that is twisted slightly to one side or the other as it is hammered will develop an uneven cross section. Forging evenly on both sides of the steel (i.e., keeping the stock square while forging) helps to avoid this. When the stock does get out of square, it will sometimes form a parallelogram (fig. 71). To fix this, place the hot iron flat on the anvil and direct the far edge of the parallelogram edge with glancing blows toward the center of the bar. Turn the bar over and repeat this step on the other side, forging its outer edge into the centerline of the stock. Then begin to hammer the bar back into a square configuration.

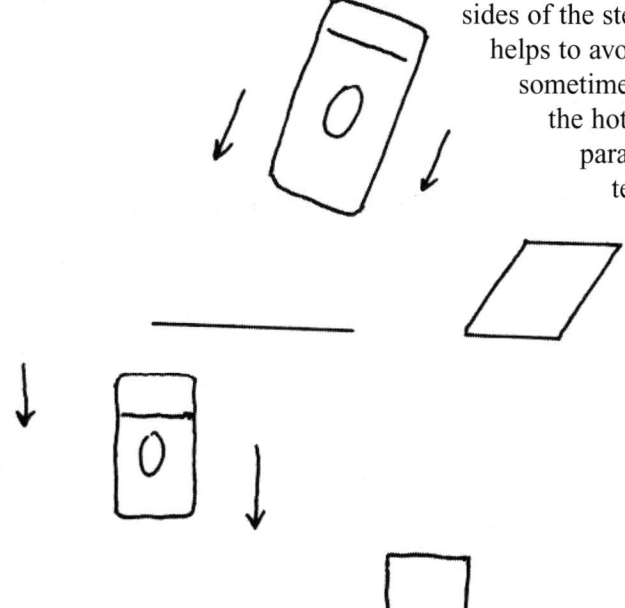

**Figure 71. Fixing parallelograms.**

### GETTING BURNT

Iron and steel that is overheated will become burned. Trying to repair or further work burned steel is wasted effort, and the burned section should be cut from the end of the bar and discarded. Keep in mind the temperature range of the steel you are working, and if you burn the steel, remember to work it at a lower heat range next time. Burning steel could also be an indication that your fire has exhausted fuel in the bottom layer, or that clinkers have formed in the bottom of the fire pot. If you are forging stock that is ostensibly low-carbon steel and you find it burning at temperatures that previous iron was worked without mishap, it could very well be that you have inadvertently been forging a bar of high-carbon steel. A quick hardness test will indicate if this is the case.

## SPLITSVILLE

Low-carbon steel is not likely to split in the process of forging unless it has been either overheated or folded over on itself as it is forged. Rather than put the effort into fixing projects gone wrong, take time to inspect the stock you buy for indications of poor manufacturing, such as folds and seams put into the steel during milling.

Wrought iron, on the other hand, because it has a grain due to a certain amount of silica inherent to its structure, is prone to splitting. It is especially prone if it is either red short or hot short (i.e., containing impurities from phosphorus or sulfur), the former being likely to split when forged at red heat and the latter prone to split at higher forging heat. The best way to check for these impurities is to forge a sample at different temperatures to see how the iron responds. If you have good wrought iron, you can avoid splitting simply by working the bar hot.

## CRACKING UP

Iron and steel that is poorly manufactured can have imperfections in the bar that might lead to cracks in the forging. With low-carbon steel, cracks are likely caused by overheating, followed by attempts to salvage the steel by reforging. Overworking the metal is futile, and it's best to abandon the damaged piece and start fresh.

High-carbon steel is more likely to develop cracks if it is forged at too low a heat; these cracks are generally not obvious and only become evident after the steel has been hardened and tempered. The polished surface then shows up very fine fracture lines that will prove to be weak areas where the steel will break when it is subjected to use. Since working high-carbon steel at lower temperatures increases the risk of cracking, avoid the temptation to work steel whose glow has faded to black. Instead, reheat the steel to the proper working temperature before proceeding.

## GETTING BENT

Unwanted bends usually develop as you forge when you heat more of the length of an iron bar than you intend to shape. Keep your heat localized to where you need it so the metal that *can* bend is the metal you *intend* to bend. Holding the bar so that it is angled up or down will also contribute to unwanted bends, as will hitting the bar in the wrong place.

## GETTING TWISTED

Hitting the hot iron with more force on one side than the other will start to twist it in the direction opposite to the force applied. Even force to the hammer blows from one side to the other will help prevent this condition. The iron can be trued up by applying more force to the other side of the twist, or the piece can be locked in the vise and untwisted with the aid of tongs.

## SHEARLY TWISTED

Hot iron and steel can only be twisted so far before it will break off. It actually twists itself off in a cutting motion. To get a feel for how much a bar can be twisted before breaking, simply practice: heat a bar, secure one end, and twist until the bar shears off. Doing this a few times will give you a tactile sense of when you should stop, as well as a visual image of how dense your twist can get before shearing occurs. Testing your stock at different temperatures will give you a fuller understanding of how far you can go under different forging conditions. Then back off on the number of twists, which will probably give you a better aesthetic result as well.

Twisting cold stock greatly increases the likelihood of twist shear. This happens because twisting cold stock causes compression in the steel, just as hammering cold steel increases its surface density. Both of these effects can be termed work hardening. Work hardening by

## Troubleshooting

twisting cold steel increases the steel's brittleness and makes it more prone to twisting off.

### CURVES AHEAD

Steel that is compressed more on one side than the other will curve away from the area thus compressed. Be careful to work the metal evenly. Alternating blows from one side of the work to the other will prevent this problem.

### HARD WORK

Iron that is worked cold will begin to become more densely packed, springy, and glossy. Too much cold hammering finally makes the iron brittle, and hammering beyond a certain point will cause it to crack and split. To prevent this, simply bring the metal back up to the proper forging heat. Cold metal requires far more hammering than hot metal. Cold hammering is hard on you and your stock, so do yourself and your materials a favor and forge your work at the proper temperature.

### LONG DRAWN-OUT AFFAIRS

It is sometimes difficult to judge how much mass is needed to draw steel out. When too much material is heated and hammered out, you get a much longer piece than you wanted. When trying to draw points, especially short, acute points, they can end up much longer than intended if one neglects to lift the bar slightly. Even if your hammer is coming down at the right angle for an acute point, because the stock is flat on the anvil, it is drawing the stock as opposed to compressing it into the finite 45-degree space supplied by lifting the bar and reflecting that angle with the hammer.

This is a problem that even experienced smiths can encounter. If you keep getting longer work than you intended, pay attention to how much stock you're using and how much you're hammering it. Step back either the amount of material or the length you're imparting to it by hammering and you should find yourself getting just what you want.

### STAYING COOL

Working in front of the forge is hot, dirty work, and it is easy to overheat. A good way to cope with this is to drink plenty of water. The summer heat adds a special challenge, and, as athletes have discovered, you need to replace electrolytes.

There is a drink blacksmiths have used for years to stay hydrated called switchel. The recipe I have used is a gallon of water with about 6 tablespoons of honey dissolved in a half cup of cider vinegar. Add the dissolved honey and cider to the water to suit your taste. It really seems to make a difference on a hot day.

If your neighbors won't be troubled by the noise, working at night or the early morning has the advantage of being the coolest times of day.

Another trick to stay cool is to pour a bit of rubbing alcohol on a small hand towel and use it to swab the sweat from your head and face. Just be sure to keep the alcohol away from your eyes, as it will sting worse than the sweat you're trying to gain relief from. An alcohol-soaked cloth, though cooling, is extremely flammable and, if left near open flame, might quietly ignite while you're not looking. The spectacle of you trying to wipe the sweat from your sweltering, fevered brow with a blazing rag might be uproariously funny to some, but chances are it would be decidedly uncomfortable for you!

# CHAPTER 7

# Projects

The projects in this chapter will help hone hammer control and coordination, as well as develop some of the basic hammer blows common to smithing. Some of the projects will help teach tong control and coordination between tong and hammer use. Each smith will find what works best for him in terms of hammer handle lengths, weight of tongs, etc.

Hardening and tempering will be employed in very basic projects. Unless specific directions are given about quenching or tempering, it is best to simply set the finished piece on a noncombustible surface to slowly normalize to room temperature. This technique is best for mild steel and general forgings.

The stock sizes for these projects are recommendations; they are by no means hard and fast requirements. Variation in the size of stock will change the finished size of a workpiece. Just keep in mind that making a piece too big or too small will increase the difficulty of the project.

The first set of projects is presented to augment the tools available to you; these tools can be used in later projects. While most of these are simple forgings, they do require some care in the treatment of the steel, careful attention to heating, and proper hardening, tempering, and shaping with file or grinder. With tongs, you will need to employ drilling, punching, riveting, and other techniques. Each of these projects includes detailed step-by-step illustrations of the forging procedures to augment and clarify the process.

# The Book of Blacksmithing

## PUNCHES AND CHISELS

### Half-Round Punch

Material: ¾-inch round stock, 60-point carbon steel (spring steel). Coil springs are a good source of material for this and all projects calling for 60-point spring steel.

1. Forge an extremely blunt square point.

2. Forge the square to a blunt octagon.

3. Forge the end round.

4. Grind blunt point to a smooth hemisphere and polish.

5. Heat to red and quench in oil. Use long tongs to keep hands clear of any flash fire.

6. Polish and temper to bronze, 500°F. (See "Tempering," chapter 5.)

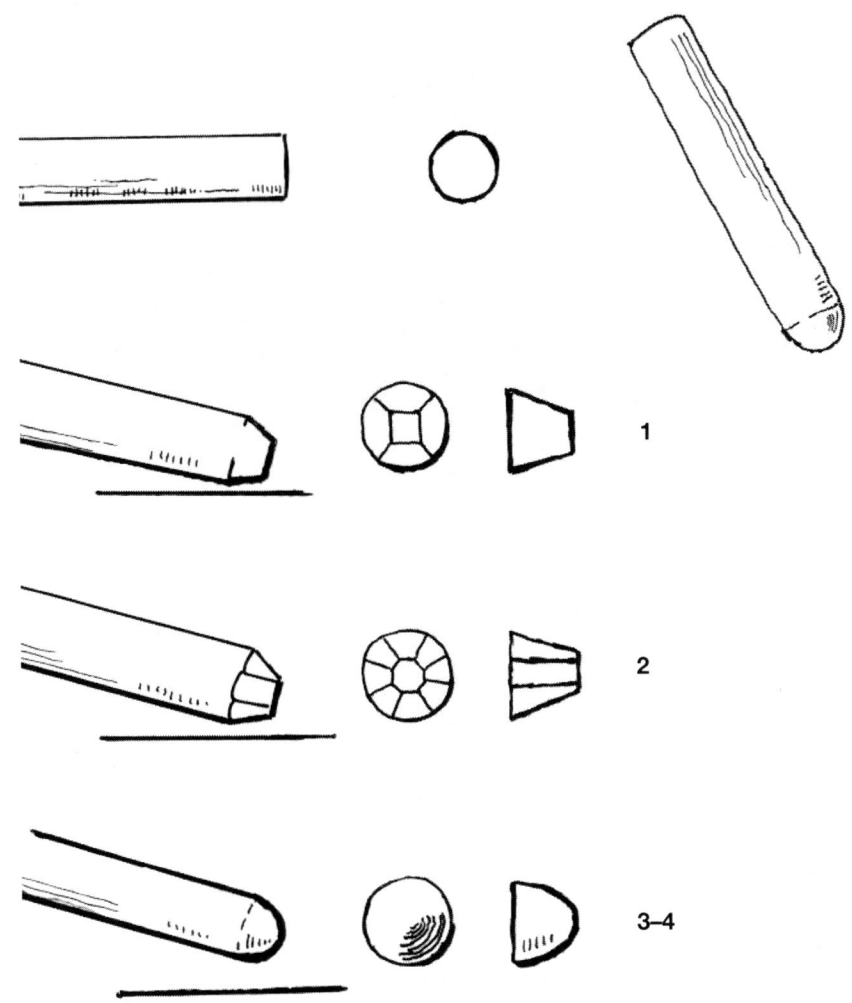

**Figure 72. Half-round punch.**

## Projects

### Center Punch

Material: ¾-inch round stock, 60 point carbon steel (spring steel).

1. Forge a sharp square point.

2. Forge the square to octagonal.

3. Forge the octagon to round.

4. Grind the center punch sharp and slightly convex.

5. Heat to a dull red and quench in oil. Use long tongs to keep hands clear of any flash fire.

6. Polish and temper to bronze, 500°F. (See "Tempering," chapter 5.)

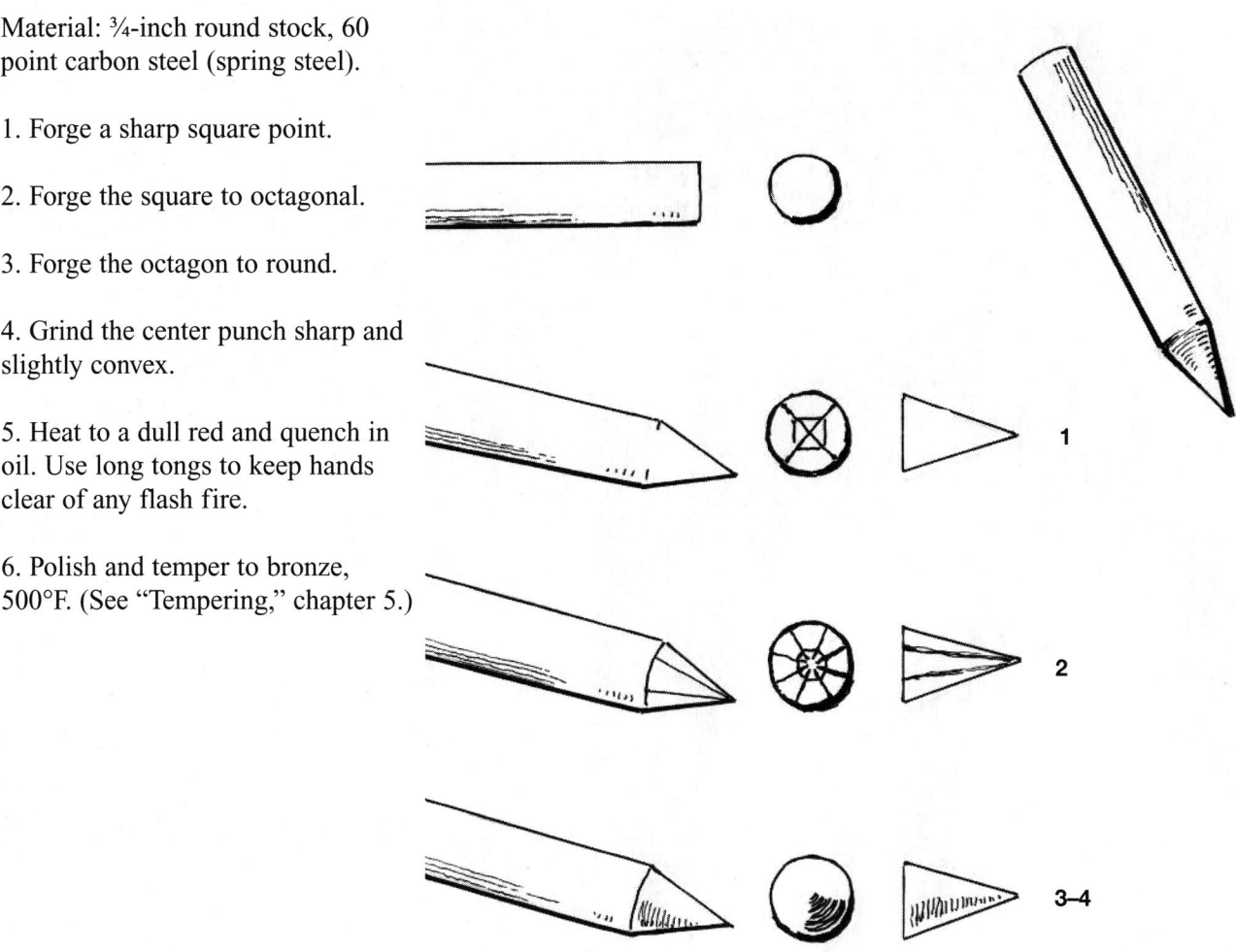

Figure 73. Center punch.

# The Book of Blacksmithing

## Eye Punch

Material: ¾-inch round stock, 60-point carbon steel (spring steel).

1. Forge a blunt square taper.

2. Set on the diamond and forge down to an octagonal section.

3. Forge round.

4. Set in vise hot and mark the center with a center punch.

5. Reheat to red, set in vise, and punch the center mark to a half-round divot with a ball punch.

6. Grind so the divot is surrounded by even walls.

7. Burnish edges with a wire brush.

8. Heat to red, quench in oil. Use long tongs to keep hands clear of any flash fire.

9. Polish and temper to blue, 560°F. (See "Tempering," chapter 5.)

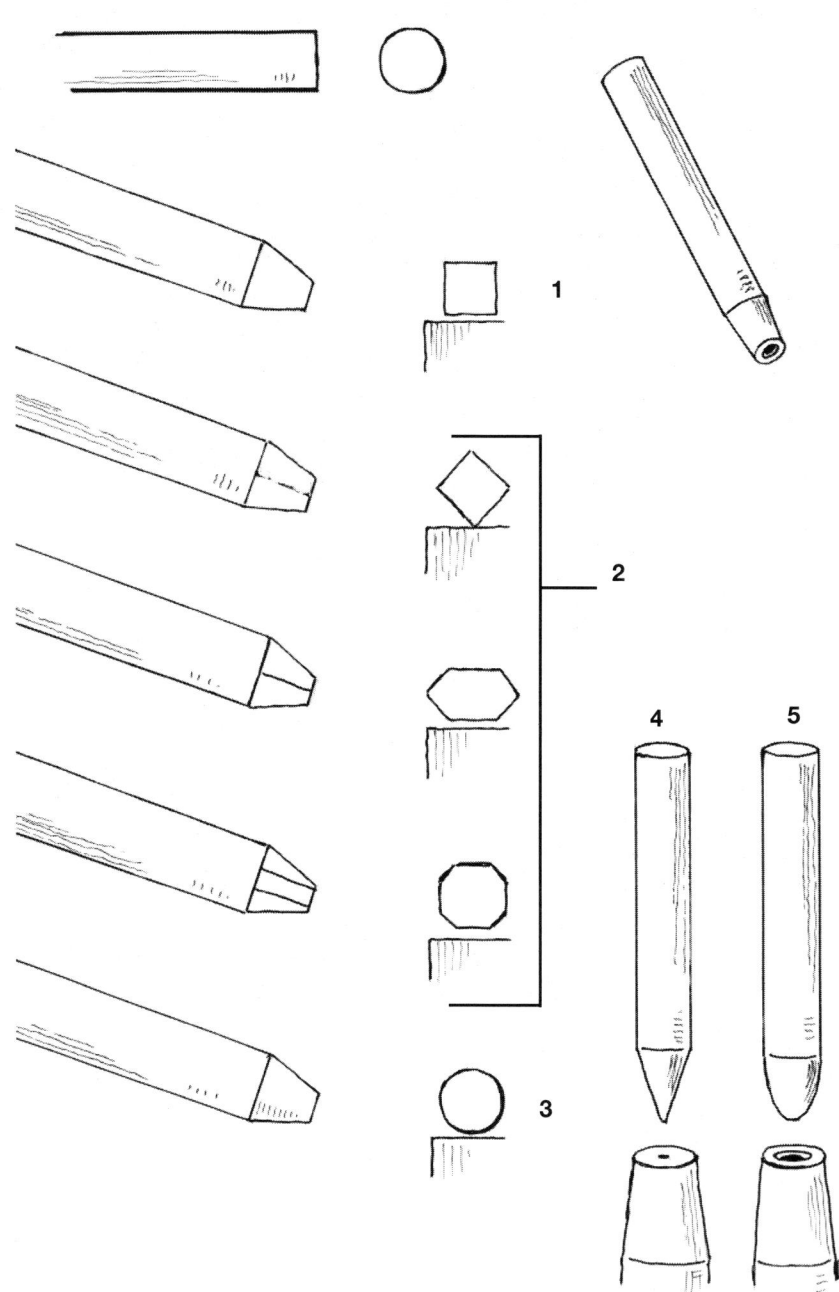

Figure 74. Eye punch.

## Projects

### Slit Chisel

Material: ½-inch round stock, 60-point carbon steel (spring steel).

1. Take the steel to a good red forging heat, being careful not to overheat. Forge a flat taper, turn 180 degrees, and repeat until chisel edge is tapered to an edge.

2. Keep the sides of the chisel blade from flaring out too much by forging in from the sides.

3. Sharpen the chisel on a grinding wheel.

4. Heat to a red heat and quench the chisel in oil. Use long tongs to keep hands clear of any flash fire.

5. Grind the edge to a slightly convex contour, which will allow the chisel blade to free itself when in use.

6. Temper the edge to reddish brown, 520°F. (See "Tempering," chapter 5.)

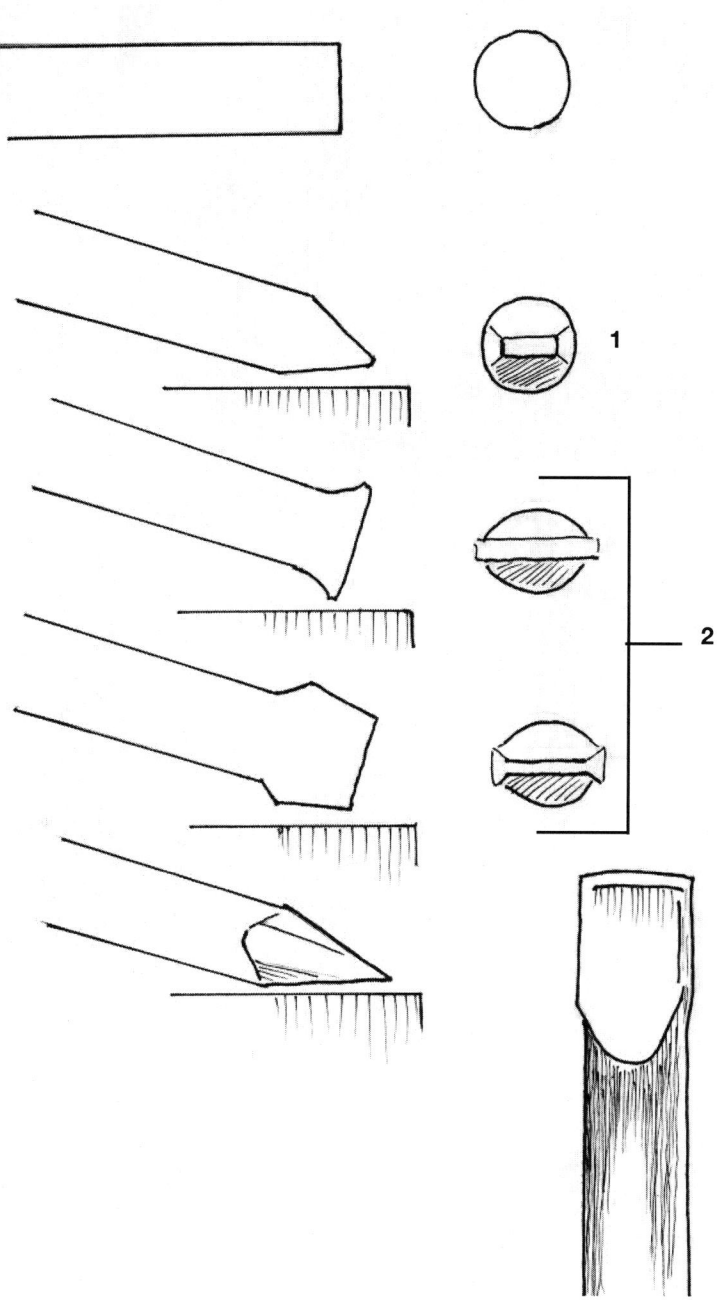

Figure 75. Slit chisel.

## The Book of Blacksmithing

### Square Taper Chisel

Material: ½-inch round stock, 60 point carbon steel (spring steel).

1. Take a good orange forging heat on the very end of a 6-inch section. Forge the end of the bar to a square cross section with a slight taper to the handle.

2. Anneal. (See "Annealing," chapter 5.)

3. File to true.

4. Heat to red heat and quench in oil. Use long tongs to keep hands clear of any flash fire.

5. Temper to purple, 540°F. (See "Tempering," chapter 5.)

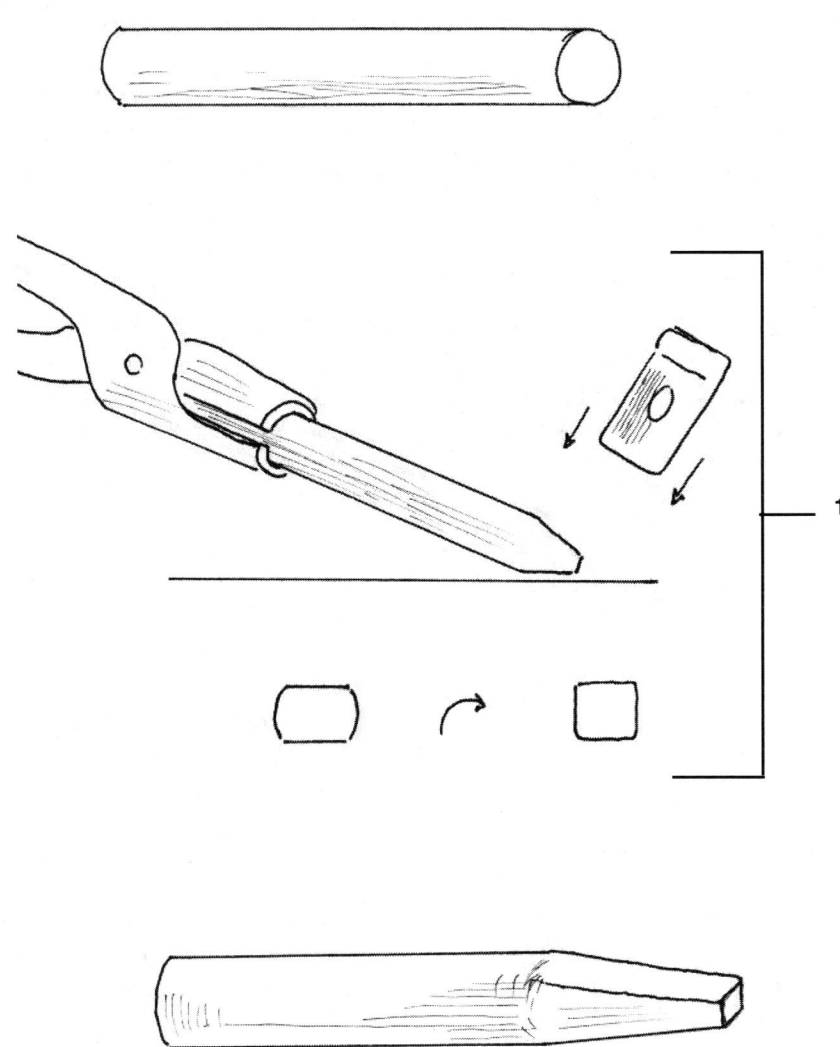

Figure 76. Square taper chisel.

76

**Projects**

**Hardy Chisel**

The hardy chisel is a very simple forging. The difficulty comes in forming large-diameter stock of medium- to high-carbon steel. You can purchase medium- to high-carbon steel bar stock new from a steel supplier. Alternatively, excellent hardy tools can be forged from salvage steel scrap. Jackhammer points are excellent steel; plus, they have an integral collar that makes an excellent hardy tool. Large coil springs with a diameter greater than the hardy hole of your anvil are also useful for this project. If using a bull point or jackhammer bit, try to obtain a size close to your hardy hole to save effort. If such a bit is not available, use square stock 1 ¾ inch or larger, at least greater than the diameter of your hardy hole. Use medium- or high-carbon steel.

1. Take the steel to a good orange forging heat. If you aren't starting with a collared bit already, forge a square tenon onto one end of the stock over the edge of the anvil. The tenon should have a slightly tapered, square cross section; this becomes the tang of the hardy tool. Check the fit in the hardy hole. You want easy insertion/removal of the tang without binding, but snug enough to be stable without the tool rocking or shifting with use.

2. Once the tang is formed, cut off enough stock above the collar to leave you with a cutting block of 3 to 4 inches (at least twice the length of the stock thickness).

3. Take a good orange forging heat and, with a heavy hammer, forge an abrupt chisel edge.

4. Anneal the hardy chisel overnight. (See "Annealing," chapter 5.)

5. Lock the hardy chisel in a vise and file it to shape and a sharp edge.

6. Heat to red forging heat, quench in oil.

7. Temper to blue, 560°F. (See "Tempering," chapter 5.)

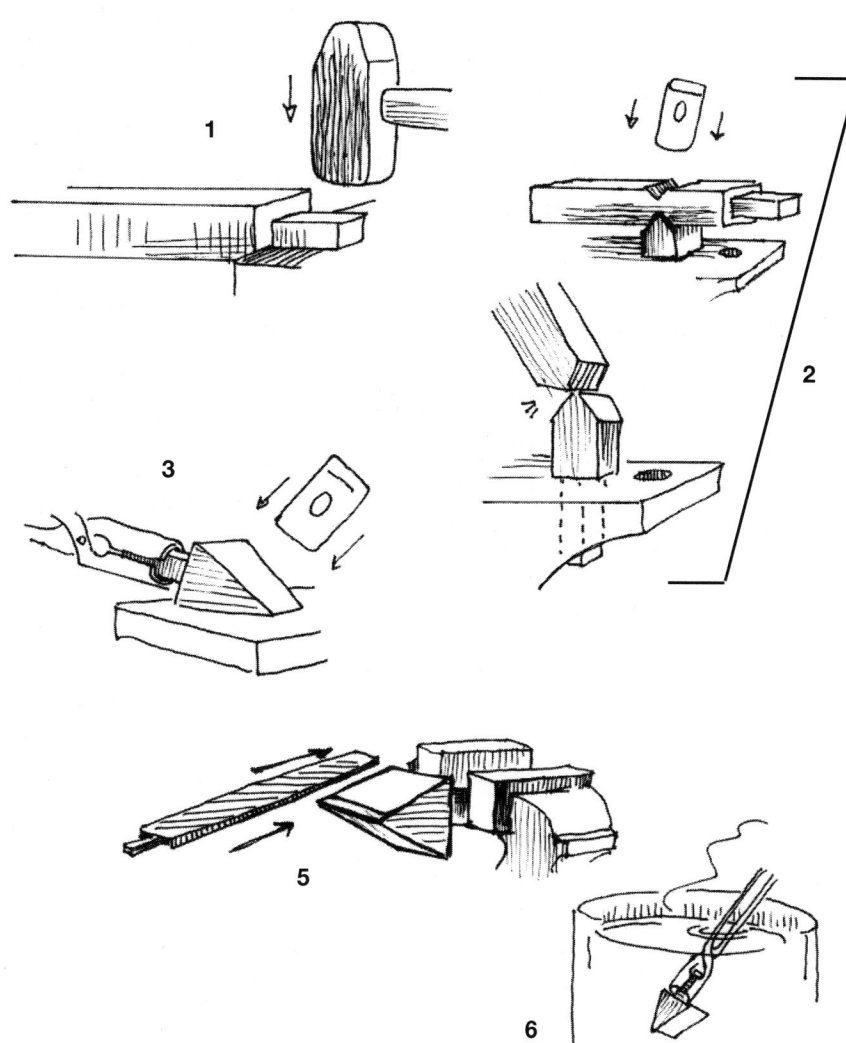

**Figure 77. Hardy chisel.**

# The Book of Blacksmithing

## OTHER FORGING TOOLS

### Quick Tongs

Material: ¼-inch x 1-inch flat bar stock, hot-rolled mild steel.

1. At a good forging heat, place steel in vise and twist 90 degrees.

2. Shoulder the tong's jaws. (See "Forming a Shoulder," chapter 5.)

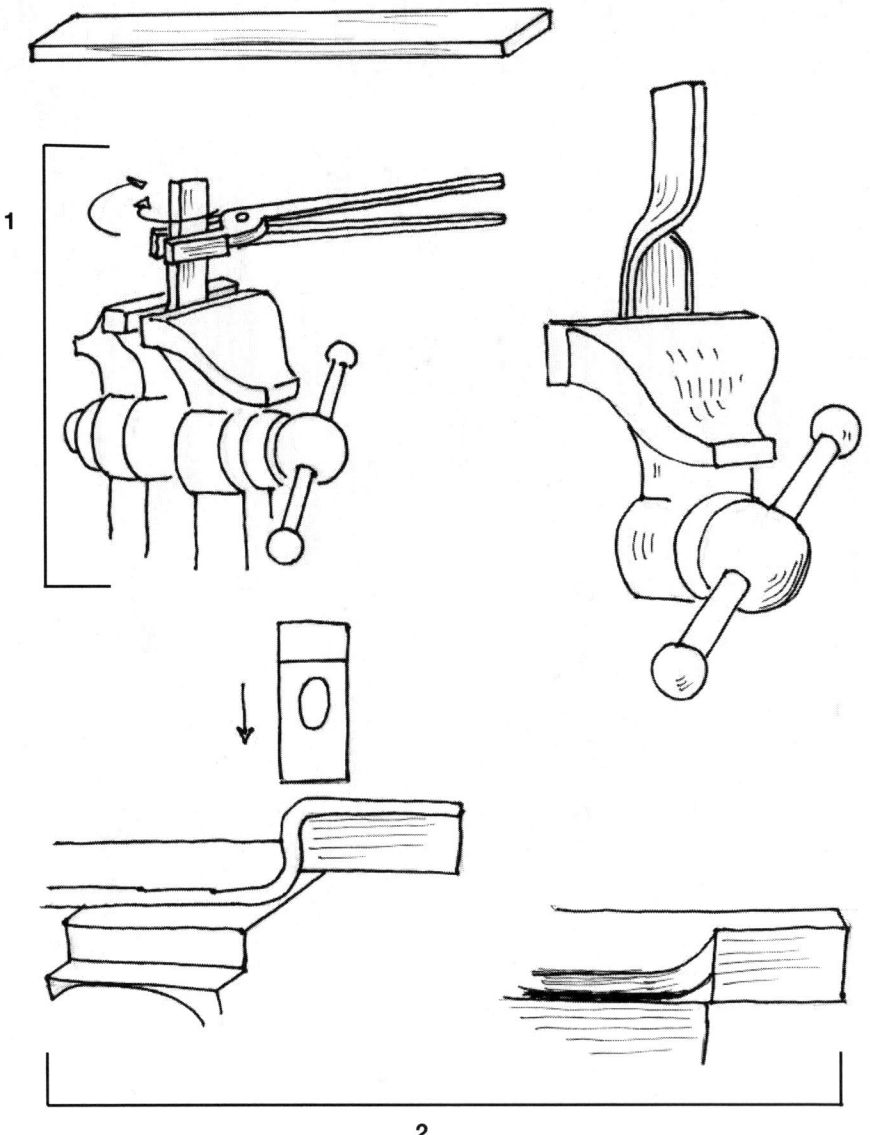

Figure 78. Quick tongs, steps 1–2.

## Projects

3. Center punch for hinge rivet hole and pilot hole to cut stock diagonally on a band saw.

4. Repeat steps 1–3 at the opposite end of the flat stock.

5. After cutting the tongs apart along the diagonal, draw out the reins to the desired length; then forge smooth.

6. Set tong hinge rivet and hot shape the jaws for tight fit and smooth working action. This involves opening and closing the jaws while the tongs and rivet are still hot.

7. Quench the tongs in water at a dull red heat, working the jaws open and closed while submerged in the water and again after you remove the tool from the water to keep the hinge working freely. If you quench the tongs without working the jaws, you risk having the tool seize too tight to open or close.

8. If you choose to use carbon steel, you must temper to a dark blue (570°F) after the quenching step or you risk breaking your tongs. (See "Tempering," chapter 5.)

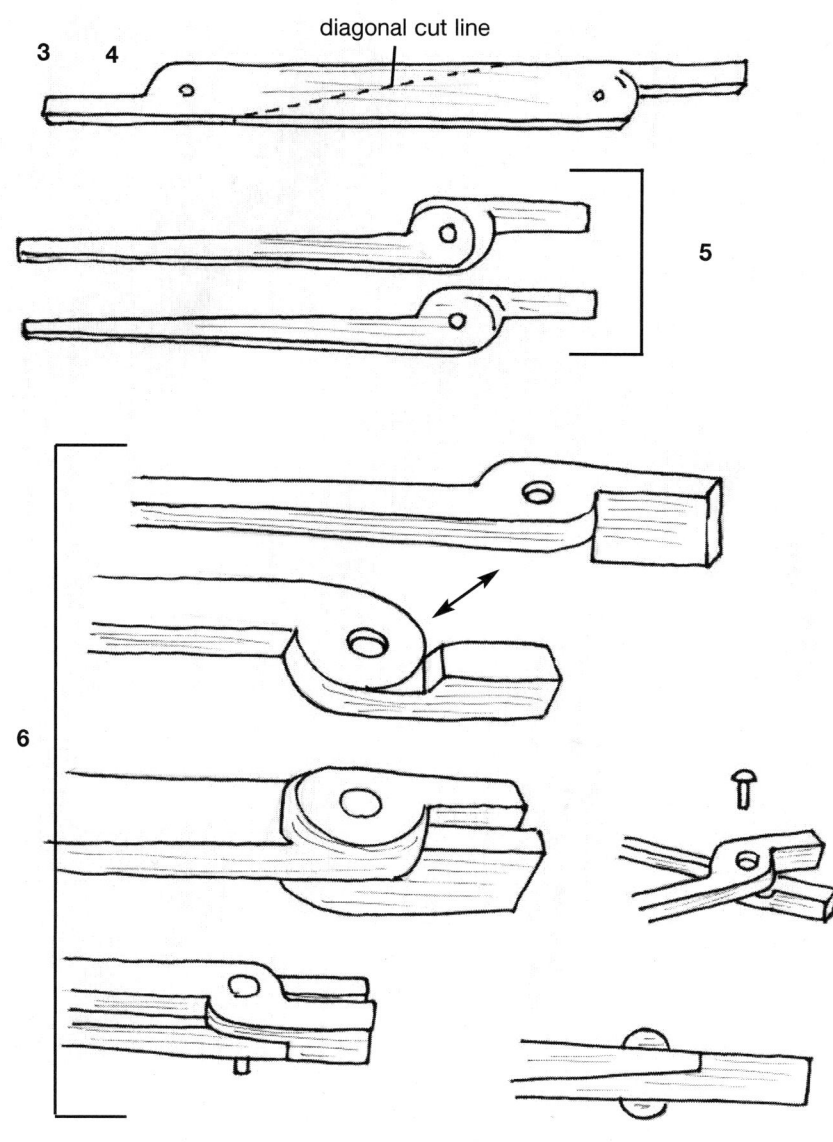

**Figure 79. Quick tongs, steps 3–6.**

# The Book of Blacksmithing

### Nail Heading Tool

Material: ¾- to 1-inch round stock, medium-carbon steel (spring steel), 8 inches long.

1. Hammer the stock along its length to flatten slightly, leaving an inch of stock at one end the original diameter.

2. Taking a good orange forging heat, extend the last inch of the bar stock over the half-rounded edge on the far side of the anvil. Shoulder the stock by hammering with the face of your hammer half over the anvil face edge and half over the overhanging stock. Do not reduce the stock more than half its thickness. This step establishes the end boss.

3. After forging the shoulder to the nail tool, invert your grip on the stock and forge a slight taper from the shoulder to the end of the bar. When the tapered rectangular cross section of the handle is forged, hammer the edges of the stock so as to leave the handle area easier to hold.

4. Once the handle area is forged to shape, heat the very end of the tapered section and extend the bar over the near edge of the anvil face. Establish a shoulder with overhanging blows of the hammer and as you slightly lift the stock with your tong hand. Lean your hammer face to reflect the angle. Turn the stock 90 degrees between hammer blows to forge a square taper.

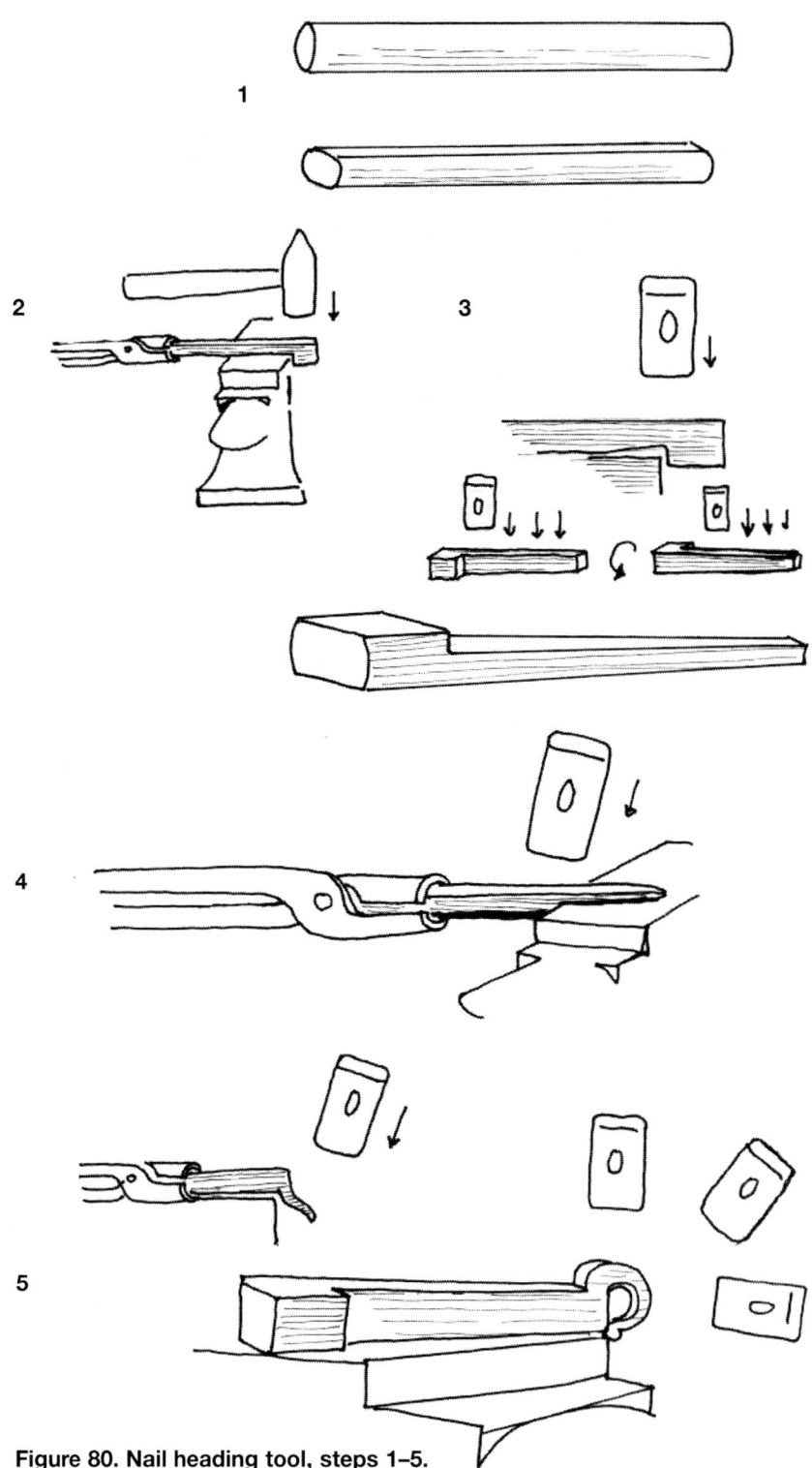

Figure 80. Nail heading tool, steps 1–5.

**Projects**

5. After forging the taper, rotate the stock 180 degrees so that the shouldered area is facing upward and extend the bar so that the area is a little beyond the far edge of the anvil. With a few glancing blows, forge the taper downward to begin forming the handle's hook. Turn the bar 180 degrees and again forge slightly down and inward as you bring the taper around and into a circular shape. The long taper has a natural tendency to form a scroll shape as it is forged.

6. Anneal the forging. (See "Annealing," chapter 5.)

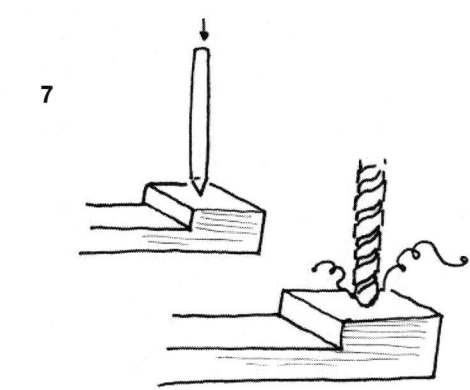

7. Center punch the boss, then drill from the top slightly smaller than the nail diameter desired.

8. Ream the bottom side of the drilled area to form a wide, tapered hole three-quarters the depth of the entire hole.

9. Using a small, square jeweler's file, file the round hole from the top until the top quarter of the hole is square in cross section. The hole should be square, but the very corners should be slightly rounded. This will help keep the nails from being wedged in place while being forged in the tool, as the slightly rounded edges are less likely to bind the nail shank. The top edge of the hole where it meets the top face of the boss should also be very slightly rounded or chamfered to help release the nail.

10. Once the nail header is formed, shape the face of the tool into a slightly convex shape. Heat the tool to a red heat and quench in oil.

11. Temper the handle to dark blue, 570°F, and the nail seat to reddish brown, 520°F. (See "Tempering," chapter 5.) Polish the convex face of the tool to help the forged nails slip out more readily as they are finished.

Figure 81. Nail heading tool, steps 7–10.

# The Book of Blacksmithing

## Riveting Hammer

Material: 1-inch square stock, medium-carbon steel (spring steel).

1. Take a good orange forging heat. Hot punch a hole about 1 ¾ inch from the end of the stock. Turn the stock 180 degrees and punch the other side.

2. Punch hole completely through bar with punch positioned over the pritchel or hardy hole.

3. Drive a drift pin into hammer eye hole. With drift in place, forge the sides of the hammer smooth.

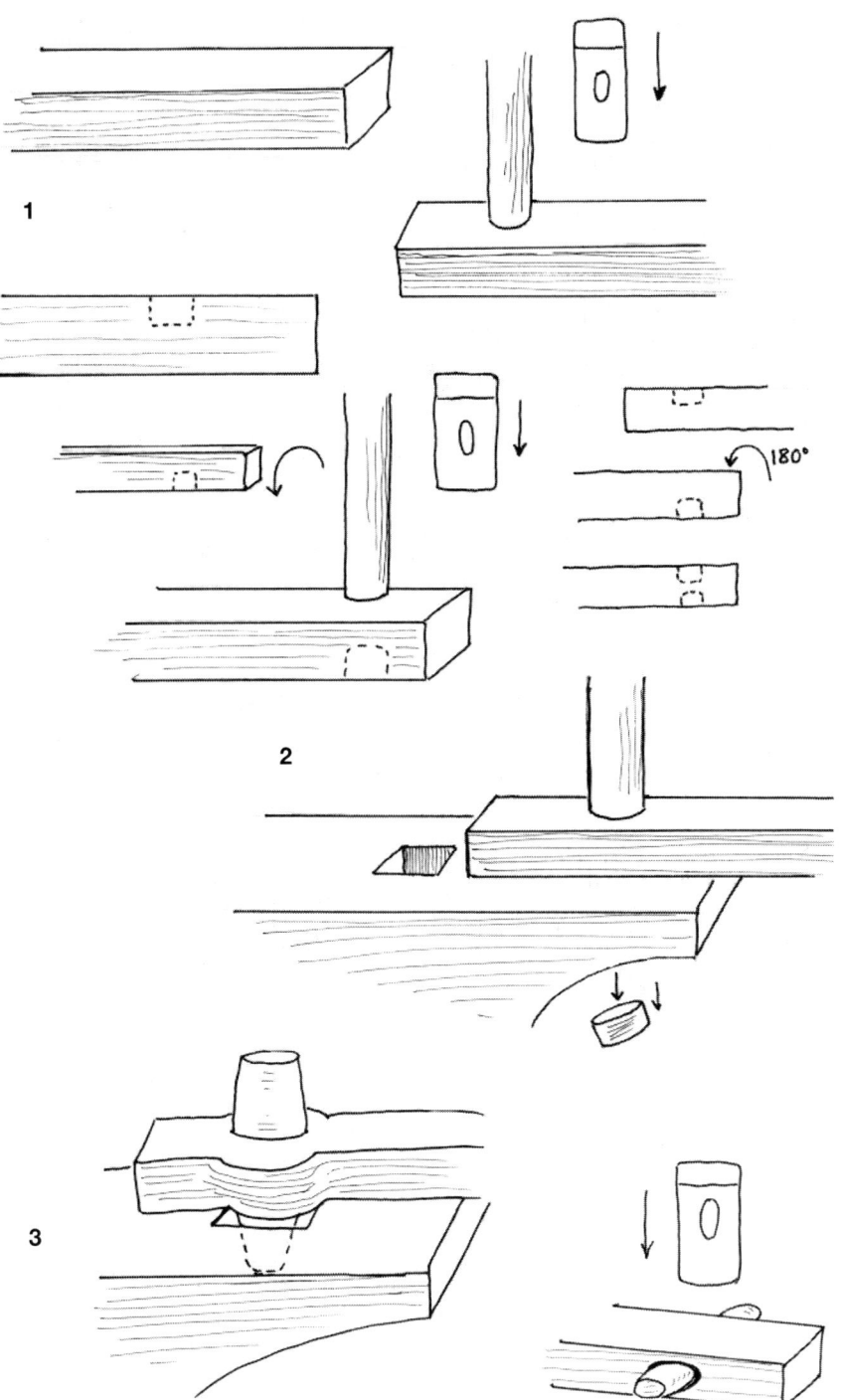

Figure 82. Riveting hammer, steps 1–3.

## Projects

4. Drive out the drift pin over the hardy hole

5. The end of the stock is the hammer's face. For about 1 inch back from the hammer's face, you will "break the edges" by resting one sharp corner edge of the square stock on the anvil while hammering the opposite corner edge to form slight chamfers. Turn the stock 180 degrees and chamfer the remaining two corner edges.

6. Hot cut the hammer off the bar using the hardy chisel, about 4 inches from the end of the stock. The end you just cut becomes the peen end of the hammer.

7. Grip the hammer through the eye with hammer tongs. Forge the peen end of the hammer to an abrupt taper.

8. Harden the tool by heating to glowing red and quenching in oil.

9. Temper to blue, 560°F. (See "Tempering," chapter 5.)

10. Add a handle of ash, hickory, white oak, or Osage. Shape the end of the handle to fit tightly and insert it into the hammerhead. Hammer in a metal wedge to tighten the handle against the head.

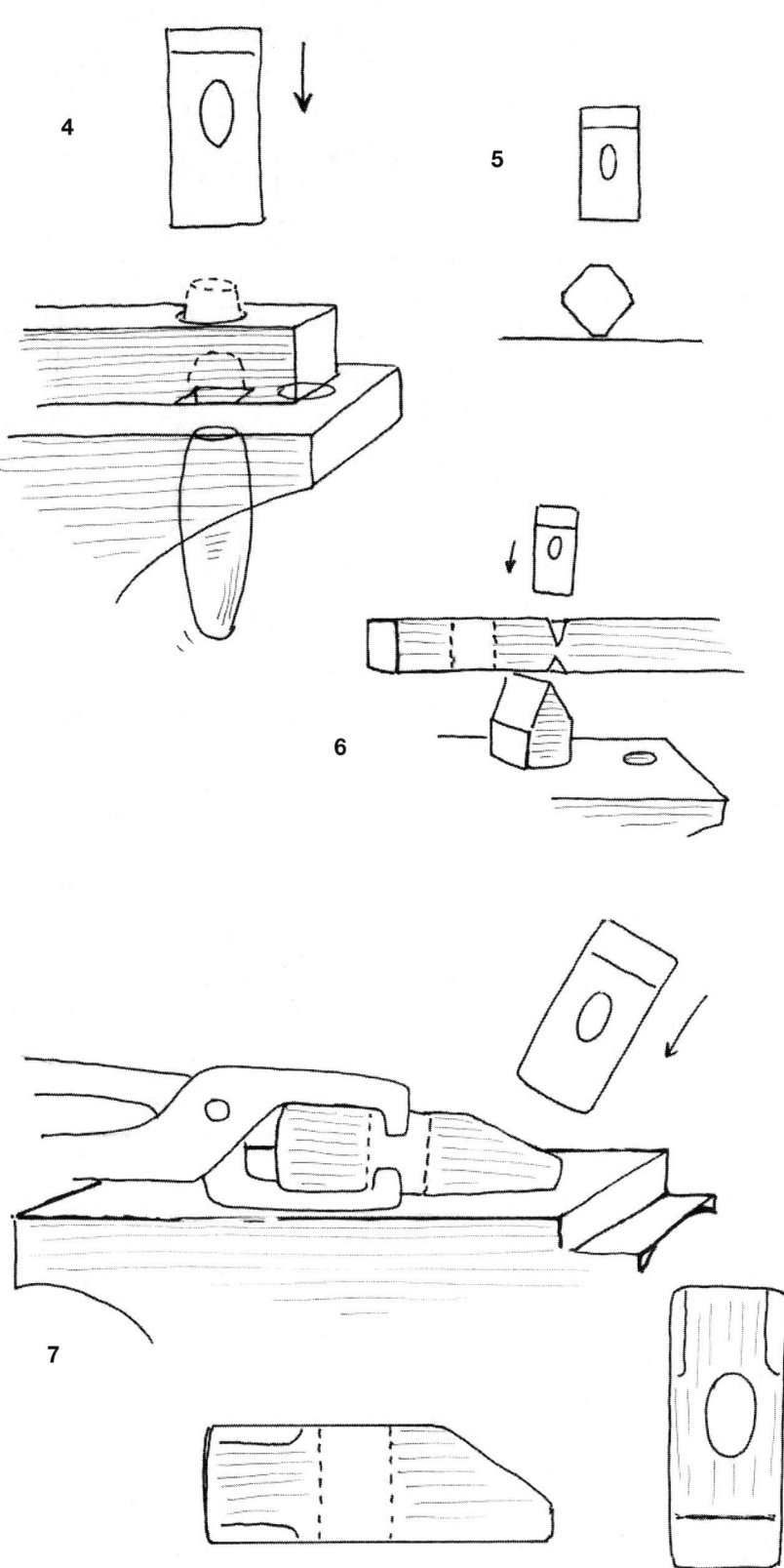

Figure 83. Riveting hammer, steps 4–7.

# The Book of Blacksmithing

## MORE PROJECTS

### Drive-In Wall Hook

Material: 3/16-inch square stock, low-carbon steel, 6 inches long.

1. Take a good orange heat. Forge a square taper at the end of the bar, then forge the taper round.

2. Using the edge of the anvil, forge the taper to a tight scroll. (See "Forming a Scroll," chapter 5.)

3. With the scroll facing upward, forge a round bend for the hook over the horn of the anvil.

4. Forge the opposite end of the rod to a sharp point, still square in cross section.

5. Grip the hook end and forge the last inch over the edge of the anvil into a right angle bend. (See "Forming a Sharp Corner Bend," chapter 5.)

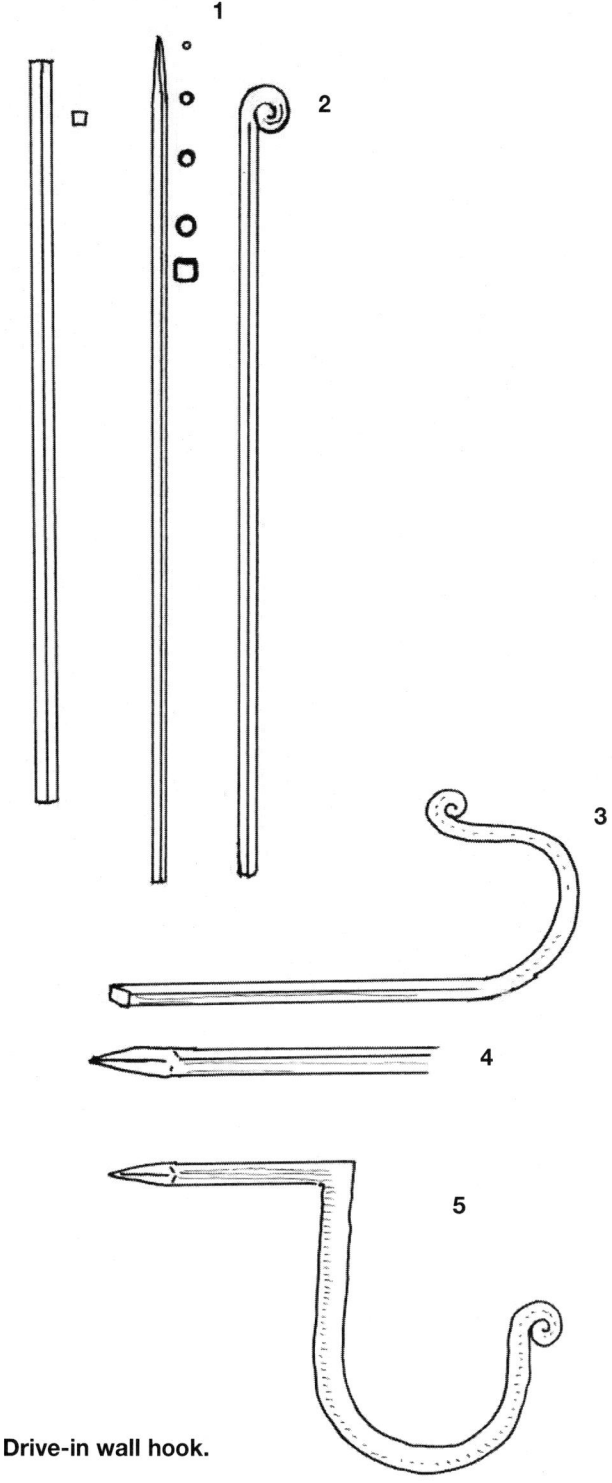

Figure 84. Drive-in wall hook.

## Projects

### S Hook

Material: 3/16-inch square stock, low-carbon steel, 8 inches long.

1. Take a good orange forging heat. Forge a square taper at both ends of the bar, then forge the tapers round.

2. Using the edge of the anvil, forge the taper at one end to a tight scroll. (See "Forming a Scroll," chapter 5.)

3. Forge another taper facing the opposite direction on the opposite end of the bar.

4. Lay the bar across the horn of the anvil with the scrolled end extending a couple inches beyond the horn and the scroll facing upward. Forge the bar down over the anvil horn to form one of the hooks.

5. Turn the stock around and turn it 180 degrees so the other scroll end is extending past the anvil horn, again with the scroll facing upward. Forge the second hook over the anvil horn. The final hook looks like an S with small scrolls at each end.

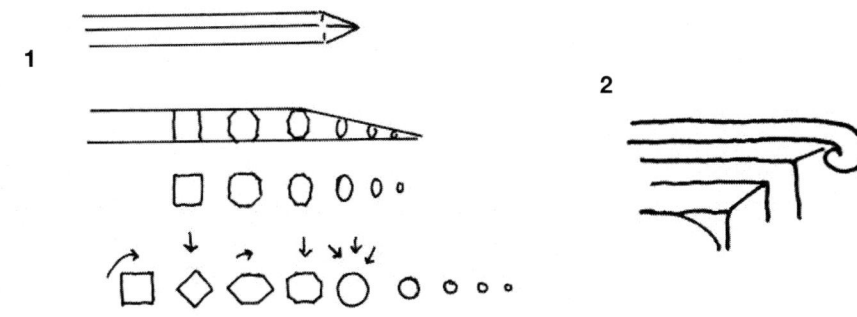
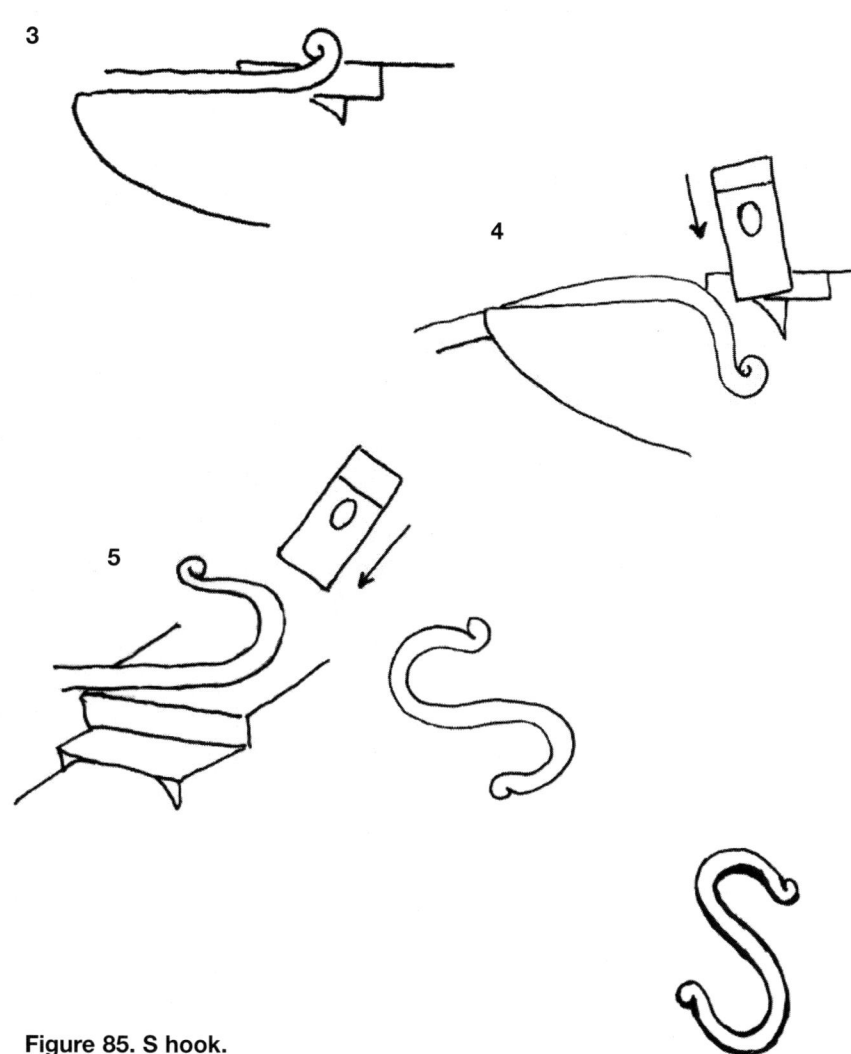

**Figure 85. S hook.**

# The Book of Blacksmithing

## Rosehead Nail

Material: ¼-inch square stock, low-carbon steel.

1. The rosehead nail is forged in one heat. Heat the stock almost to a yellow forging heat. Lay about 1 to 1 ½ inch of stock on the near edge of the anvil and forge a shoulder using overhanging blows. Turn stock 90 degrees and forge a shoulder again. This gives you a square nail shank at the end of the stock that is half the width of the stock and offset toward one corner of the bar. Continue the shouldering steps until the diameter of the shank fits the square hole of the nail heading tool.

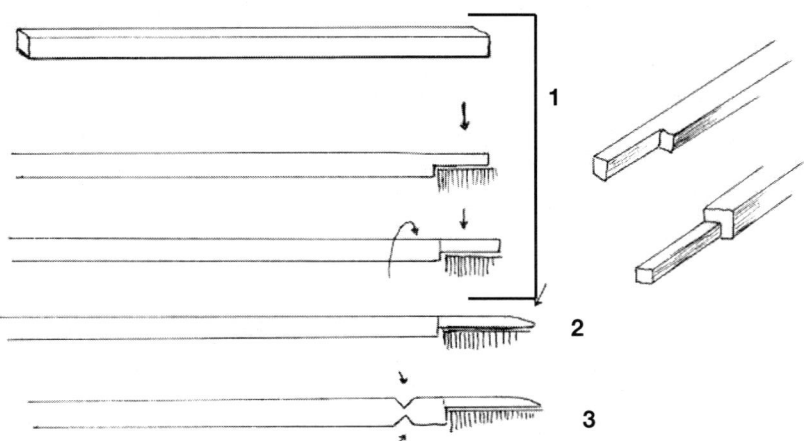

2. Forge a sharp point on the end of the nail shank. (See "Forging an Acute Point," chapter 5.)

3. Using a hardy chisel, nick the stock on both sides about 3/16 inch back from the shoulder. Do not cut the nail off the bar yet; just nick it enough so you can bend the nail off once it's in the nail heading tool.

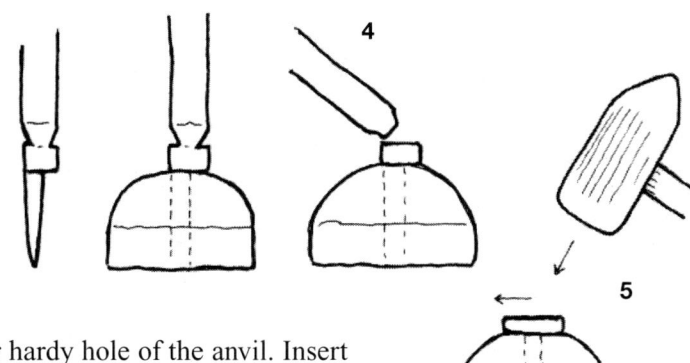

4. Hold the nail heading tool over the pritchel or hardy hole of the anvil. Insert the shank of the nail through the nail heading tool and break the nail off the bar at the point you nicked. By this time, the nail should be a red heat.

5. Your first hammer blow to the nail head should be a light tap struck at an angle to center the nail head on the nail shank. Following this, strike a smart blow on the top of the nail head to flatten it.

6. Last, strike each corner of the square nail head a glancing blow to form the petals of the rosehead.

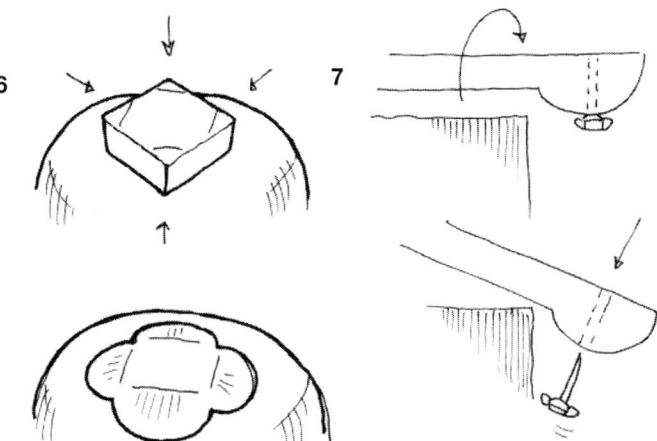

7. Turn the nail heading tool over and strike it sharply over the edge of the anvil to dislodge the nail to the ground. Although the nail will be black by now, allow it to cool for 10 minutes before attempting to pick it up.

Figure 86. Rosehead nail.

## Projects

### Horseshoe Paperweight

Material: ¼- x ½-inch bar stock, hot-rolled mild steel, 8 inches long.

1. Take a good orange forging heat. Forge the bar over the horn of the anvil into a U shape, bending first one side and then the other.

2. Set a small stake anvil in the hardy hole. Hold the horseshoe securely in a pair of clip-jaw tongs and bring one arm of the horseshoe to a good orange forging heat.

3. Extend the arm over the edge of the stake anvil about ½ inch and strike to bend it down into a toe calk shape. Use overhanging blows first down and then in at an angle.

4. Hold the other arm of the horseshoe in the clip-jaw tongs, reheat to orange heat, and forge the other toe calk.

5. Turn the horseshoe 90 degrees, fit over the edge of the anvil, and square up the ends with light hammer blows. Set aside and allow to cool to room temperature.

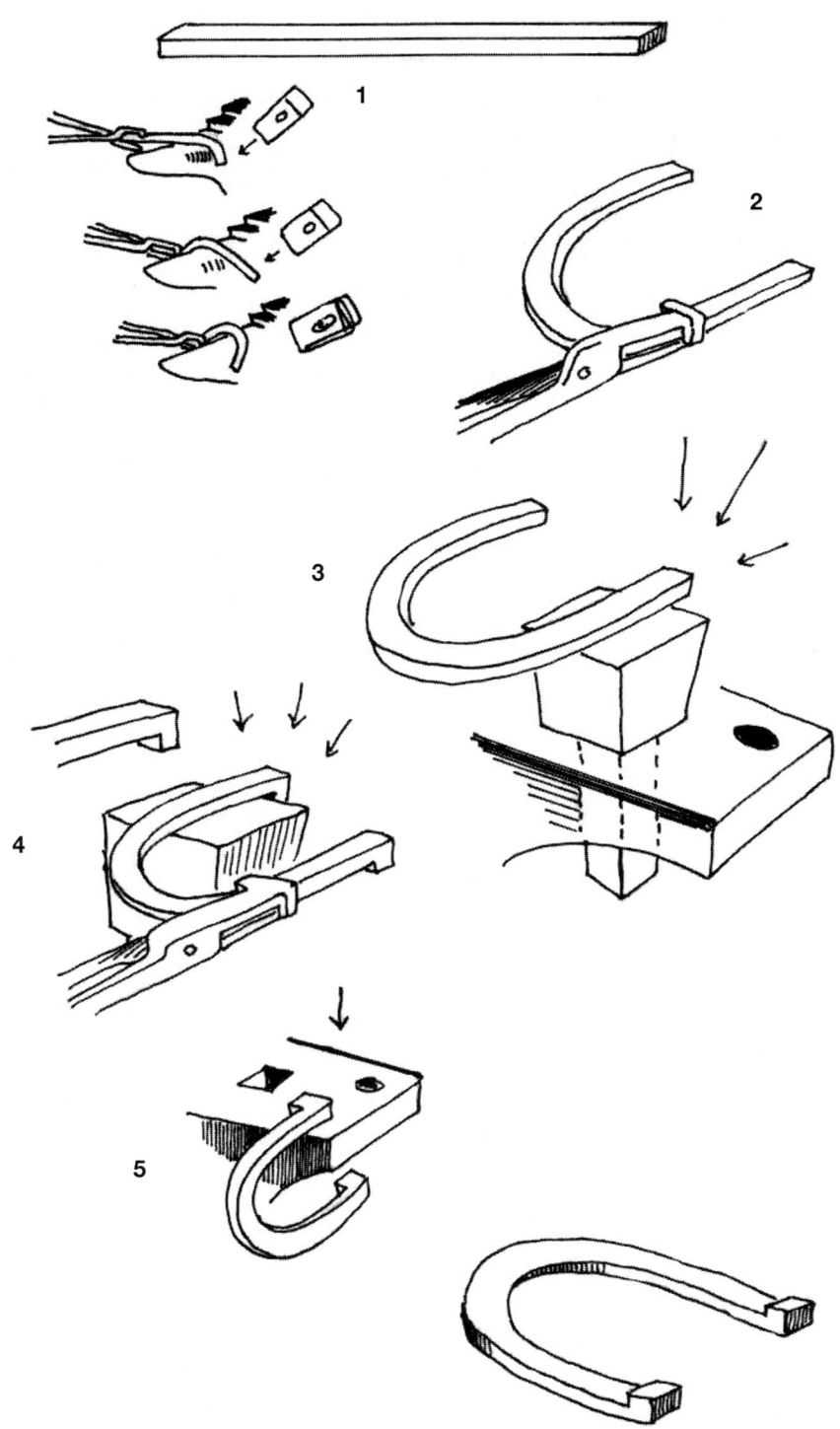

Figure 87. Horseshoe paperweight.

## The Book of Blacksmithing

### Heart Trivet

Material: ¼ x ½-inch bar stock, hot-rolled mild steel, 16 inches long.

1. Center punch the edge of the bar to mark the halfway point.

2. Heat just the very center of the bar to a good orange heat. Pound the end over the anvil's horn into the beginning of a U shape, with the broader dimension forming the face of the U.

3. Switch sides and complete the U shape.

4. Reheat and pound the center of the U into a V shape.

5. Heat one end of the V and lay its face (the broader dimension) onto the near edge of the anvil, ½ inch from the end of the bar. Forge a shoulder there half the thickness of the bar. Forge this shoulder into a rounded tab.

6. Flip the piece over and forge the mirror image tab at the other end of the V. The two tabs should face each other so that they will overlap to form a lap joint.

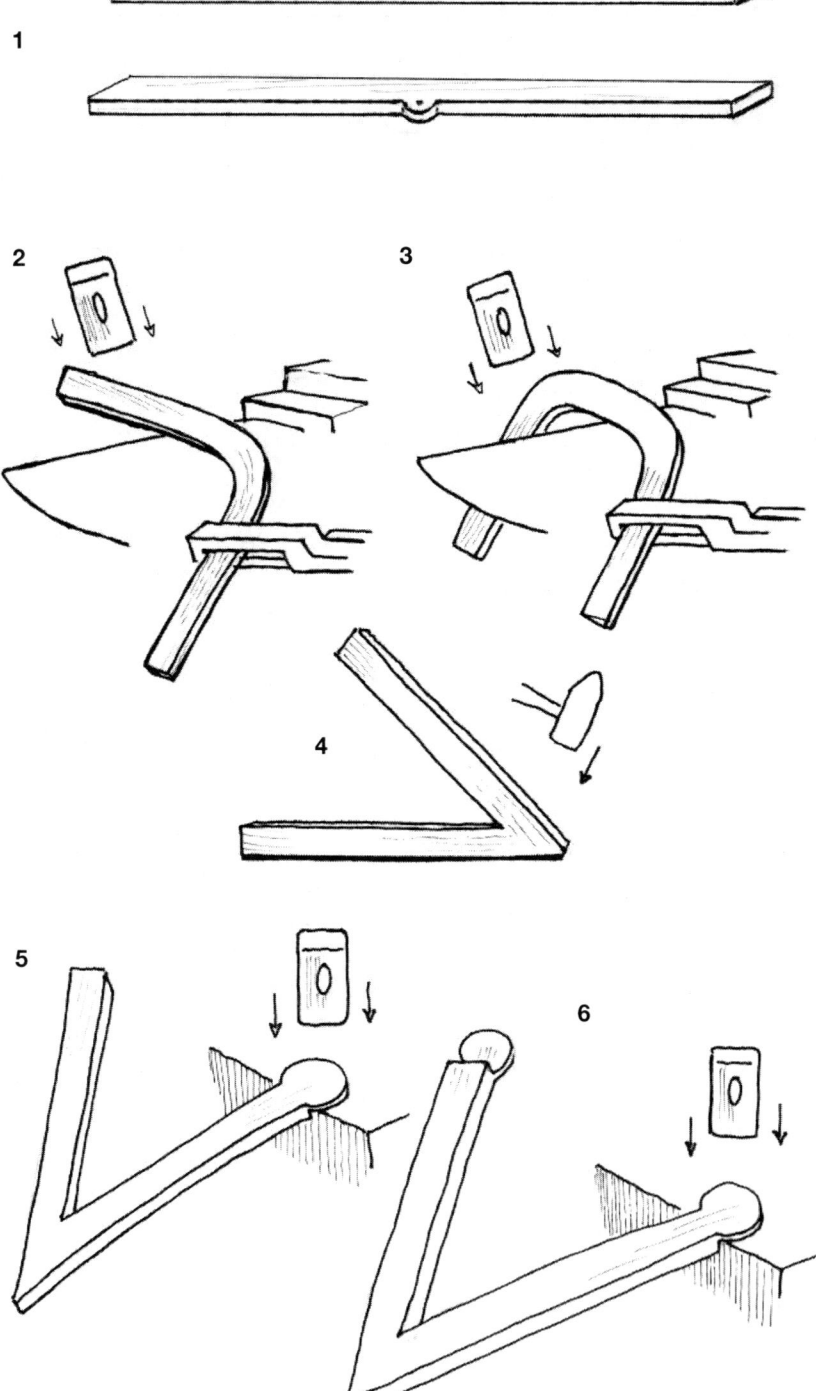

Figure 88. Heart Trivet, steps 1–6.

**Projects**

7. Heat one arm of the V and forge the arch of the heart over the horn of the anvil.

8. Switch sides and forge the opposite arch of the heart over the horn of the anvil.

9. Continue to forge the arches to bring the shouldered end tabs together. They should lap to form a combined thickness equal to the rest of the trivet.

10. Drill four ¼-inch holes, one through the lapped end tabs and three more placed in a stable triangular configuration.

11. Insert a ¼-inch diameter rivet, 5/16 inch in length, through the lapped end tabs from underneath. Using a ball-peen hammer, spread the protruding end of the rivet evenly.

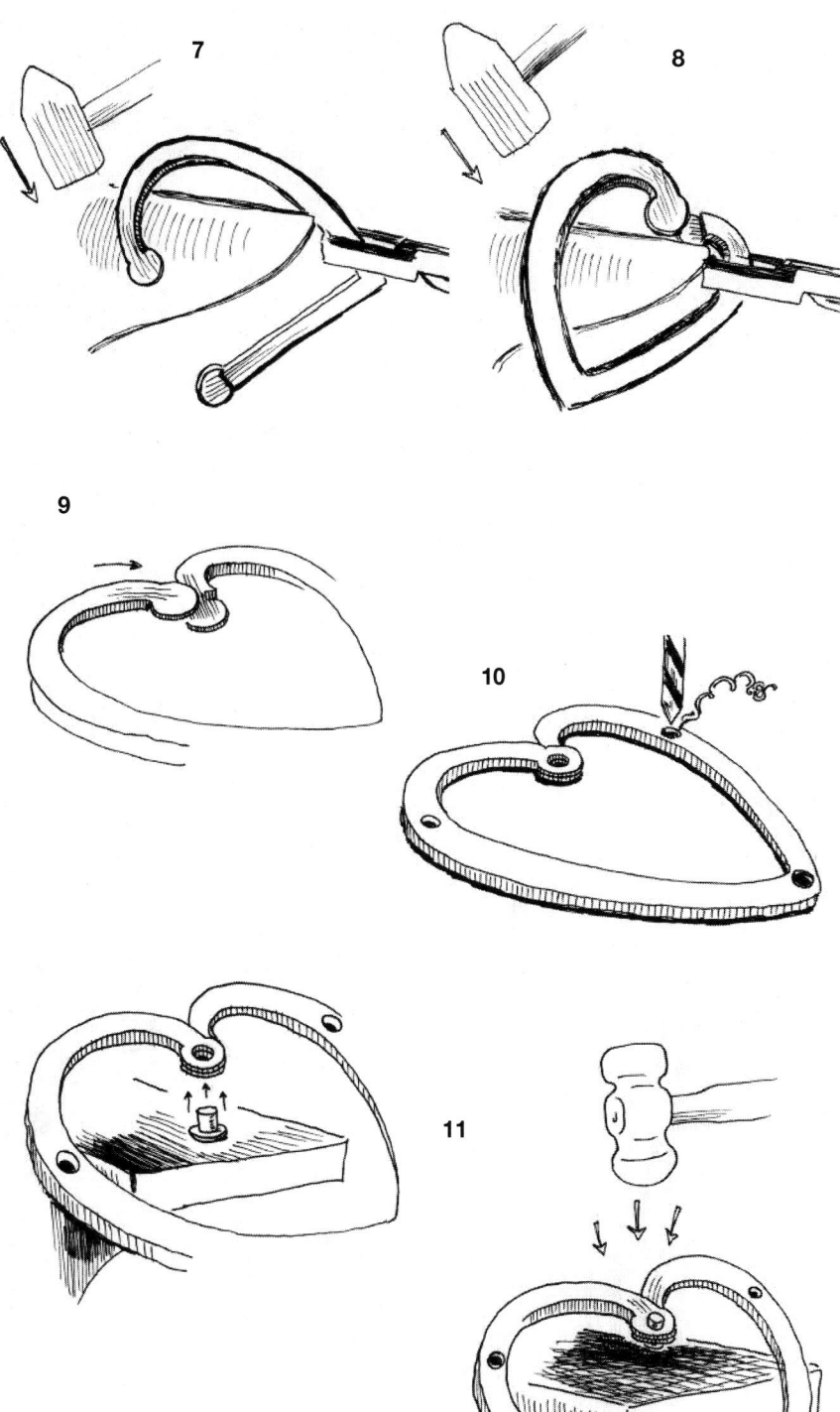

**Figure 89, steps 7–11.**

12. The three legs with penny feet are forged from 5/16-inch round stock, 4 inches in length. Forge a tenon in one end of the leg by shouldering the stock while turning it. The tenon should end up ¼ inch thick by 5/16 inch long.

13. Switch the grip with the tongs so you are holding the tenon end of the leg and forge a penny foot at the other end. (See "Forging a Penny Foot," chapter 5.)

14. Test the legs for fit and tap into the holes drilled in the trivet.

15. Lock the leg into a vise and, using a machinist's hammer, peen over the protruding ends of the tenons to rivet the feet in place.

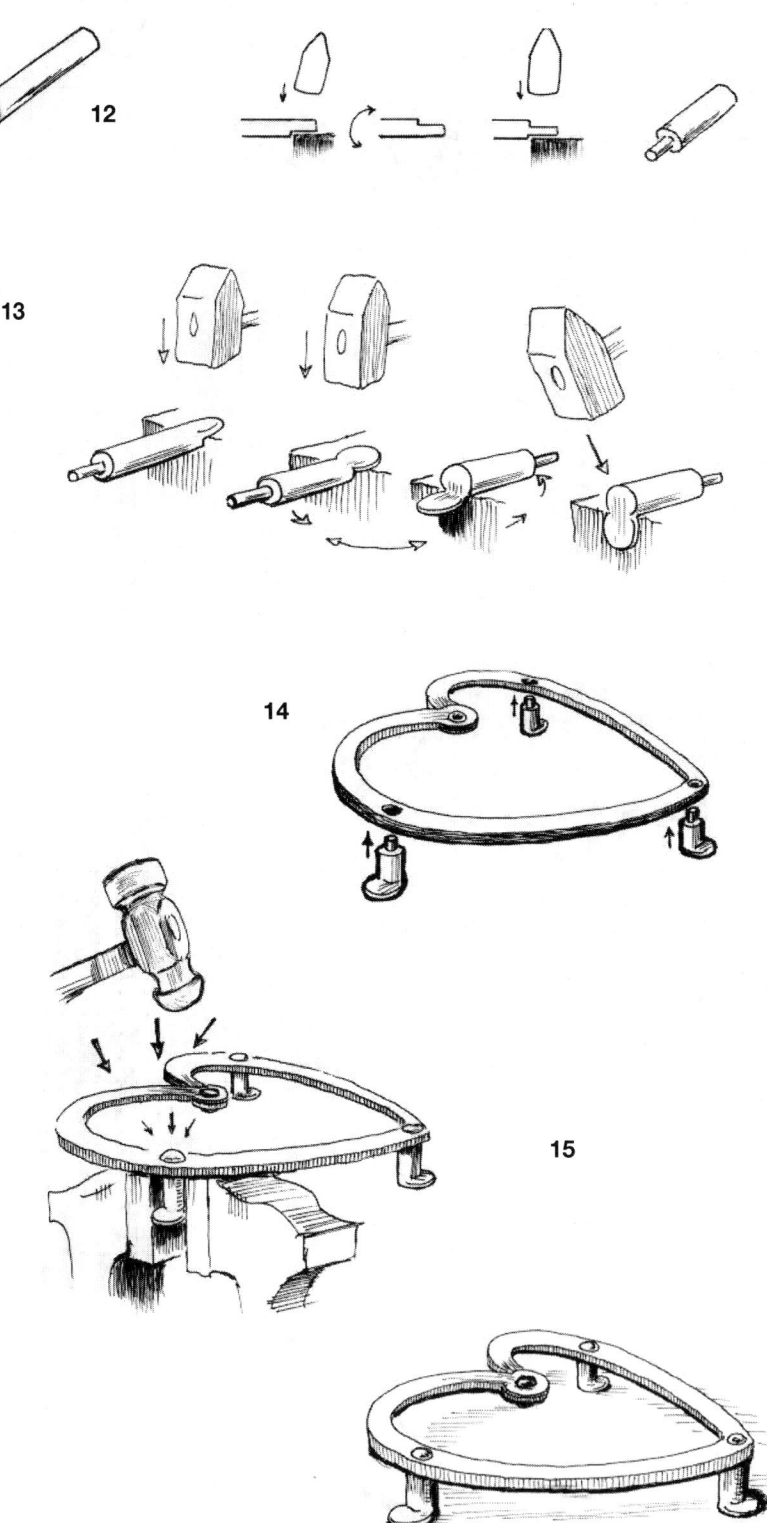

Figure 90, steps 12–15.

## Projects

### Single-Edge Knife

Material: ¼- x ½-inch bar stock, hot-rolled mild steel, 8 inches long.

1. Heat the bar so that 4 inches of the end takes a good orange heat. Shoulder one side and then the other to form a tang for the knife's handle.

2. Heat the opposite 4 inches to a good orange heat. Hold the unheated tang end with bolt tongs and forge an acute point over the face of the anvil.

3. Bring stock back up to heat and, using the horn of the anvil, bend the stock downward into a half-crescent shape.

4. Reheat blade to forging temperature and begin forging blade, alternating your blows so both sides of the blade are worked evenly. Note that as you work, the blade will gradually straighten from its downward crescent shape. Compressing a single edge will cause it to curve upward like a pirate's cutlass. The initial downward curve of the blade serves to counteract this effect. Because you're working with mild steel, you may continue to work the blade even after it has cooled somewhat. The cold hammering will help impart hardness to the metal and makes tempering unnecessary. Being mild steel, the finished blade won't be particularly hard, but it'll serve nicely for lighter duty such as a letter

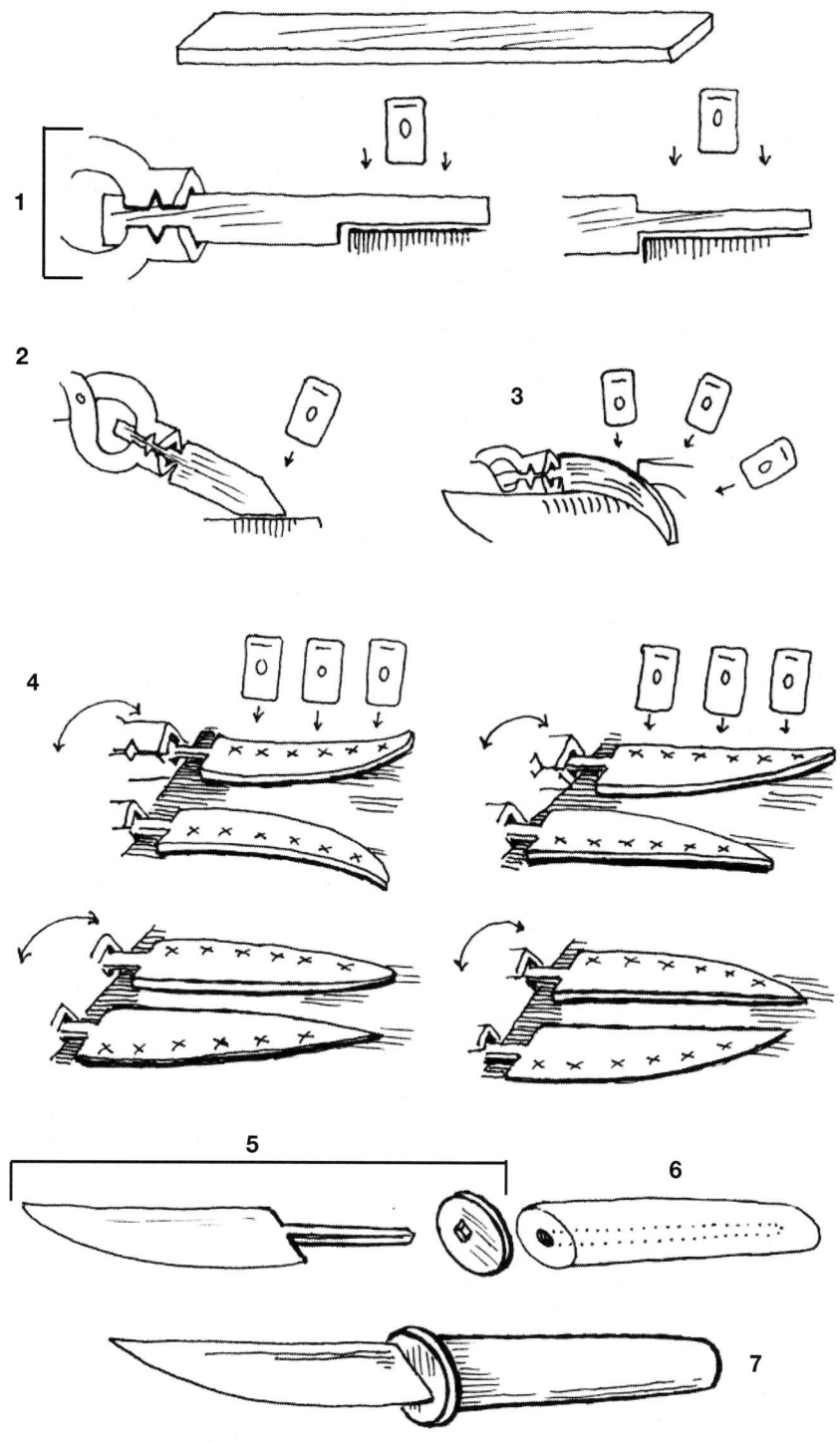

Figure 91. Single-edge knife.

opener or even as an eating utensil. Also, although it won't hold an edge for long, it'll be easy to sharpen it as needed.

5. Once the blade is formed to your liking, fit a handle to it. Make a bolster (or guard) from a soft metal such as brass by drilling and shaping with a small file. It should set snugly onto the tang, where it rests directly behind the blade. It's a good idea to make the bolster large enough to provide your hand with some protection from the blade. Drilling the opening for the tang slightly above center leaves more bolster below to act as additional protection against your hand slipping forward into contact with the blade.

6. You can use almost anything for the handle, but a good piece of hardwood or, if you can get it, a nice bit of antler are hard to beat. Shape the handle to provide a good, comfortable grip; then drill to a depth adequate to fully accept the tang.

7. Lock your blade into a vise, make sure your bolster is properly in place, and then gently tap the handle down onto the tang. The drill hole should be just large enough to accept the tang with minimal force, the idea being that the square shoulders of the tang will lock it securely into place. You can add a drop of epoxy or other suitable adhesive before inserting the tang if you like. Sharpen the blade and congratulations—you've made a knife!

# About the Author and Illustrator

**The Cardiff twins: Pat (left) and Mike. (Photo by Holly Eliot.)**

**Mike in his workshop twisting iron. (Photo by Rebecca Cardiff.)**

Author Mike Cardiff and illustrator Pat Cardiff are identical twins. Since they were born on St. Patrick's Day, their first names were a foregone conclusion. The two brothers have come a long way since their earliest blacksmithing collaboration, which involved rolling a quartzite boulder that weighed more than both of them combined to their parents' backyard for Mike to use as an anvil.

Mike developed his early blacksmithing technique working with Harry Evans and Dave Wooters at the Tidewater Foundry in Easton, Maryland. He then studied under Ken Schwarz, whom he credits with truly starting him on his career in blacksmithing. Mike later worked for several years in Colonial Williamsburg as a production smith. However, he found production work limited his opportunities to expand his knowledge of technique and decided to strike out on his own as an independent smith. Working within the Society for Creative Anachronism, Mike found an ideal environment for expanding his skills while providing an appreciative audience with accurate reproductions of medieval period tools, weapons, and utensils. He has also provided practical forging demonstrations at reenactment events and has selflessly shared his knowledge with other aspiring smiths. Mike's Damascus steel swords and knives are especially sought after by discerning blade collectors and edged weapon enthusiasts.

Mike's personal interests include rockhounding, paleontology, anthropology, and the natural sciences in general. He's a certified diesel repair mechanic, a scuba enthusiast, and has training as an EMT. He's also an avid fisherman and has been known to enjoy this particular pastime in the midst of a full blown hurricane.

A rugged individualist, Mike has pursued his craft with unwavering devotion and dedication. In the realm of metal smithing, he is an artist's artist!

When he's not painting landscapes or providing cover paintings and illustrations for books, artist Pat is usually designing, carving, and throwing boomerangs. Pat's boomerangs are crafted to resemble a wide variety of subject matter, with a strong emphasis on accurately portrayed wildlife. His fine art boomerangs have been featured in galleries across the nation. They are proudly displayed by collectors and are used in competition by throwers in the United States as well as abroad. For more information about Pat and his work, visit www.patcardiff.com.

Pat with one of his custom boomerangs. (Photo by Holly Eliot.)